HOPE FOR SOUTH AFRICA

HOPE
FOR SOUTH AFRICA

B9

ALAN PATON

FREDERICK A. PRAEGER
Publishers
NEW YORK, N.Y.

BOOKS THAT MATTER

Published in the United States of America
in 1959 by
Frederick A. Praeger, Inc., Publishers
15 West 47th Street, New York 36, N.Y.

Library of Congress Catalog Card Number: 59-7727

Printed in Great Britain in 1959 by
Taylor Garnett Evans & Co. Ltd.,
Watford and London

CONTENTS

PREFATORY NOTES

1. I have, wherever possible, spelt 'liberalism' and 'liberal' without the use of a capital letter. Occasionally, however, I have used the capital letter, and the words then refer to the more precisely formulated beliefs of the Liberal Party, and to one who espouses them. I hope this causes no confusion.

2. The word 'African' is used in this essay to denote the descendants of the original native black population. The word 'native' is used only when it is unavoidable, as in 'native reserves', 'Native Affairs Department', i.e. official terminology.

The word 'Bantu' is also used where it seems necessary, but I might inform my readers that Africans, while not objecting to the word 'Bantu', used of a language group, object to its use to describe the African people. The problem is not easy to solve, for while 'African' is the obvious analogue of 'European', it will not do when one is speaking of 'Afrikaners' and 'English-speaking' South Africans. What is one to do then? It is extremely cumbrous to enumerate all the South African tribes, such as Zulu, Sotho, Xosa, etc. etc.

CHAPTER I

INTRODUCTORY

THE political power in South Africa is almost entirely in the hands of the white people. The exceptions are that Africans are represented in the Senate by four Europeans, and in the Lower House by three Europeans, all of whom they elect; the Coloured people are represented by four Europeans, also elected by them. At one time Africans and Coloured people who were qualified to vote in the Cape Province were on the common roll, and voted like everyone else, except that the elected legislators had to be white; but General Hertzog and his United Party, aided by Dr. Malan's Nationalist Party, were able in 1936 to secure the two-thirds majority needed to remove African voters to a separate roll, and in 1956 Mr. Strijdom and his Nationalist Party manufactured a two-thirds majority by means of enlarging the Senate and removed Coloured voters to a separate roll.

Therefore today the white population of South Africa and South-West Africa is represented by 156 Members of Parliament, and the non-white population by seven members while in the Senate the numbers are eighty-five and four respectively.

The Indian people are entirely unrepresented. In 1946 General Smuts and his United Party offered the Indian people a token representation similar to that accorded to African and Coloured people, as a compensation for restrictions on Indian land and property ownership and purchase, but before the Indians could use this representation—and it is doubtful whether they would have—it was withdrawn by Dr. Malan and his Nationalist Party when they came into power in 1948. The Nationalists have always regarded the Indian population as alien and unassimilable, and intend to segregate them strictly, with the hope that this will induce them to 'return' to India. The overwhelming majority of Indians were born in South Africa, to which country the forebears of most of them were brought by the joint efforts of the sugar planters and the Government of Natal, in the latter half of last century.

Also unrepresented are Coloured women, who were never admitted to the Cape franchise, and all the Coloured people, both men and women, of the Transvaal and the Orange Free State.

That briefly is the present position. Of 252 legislators, eleven represent African and Coloured voters, but these eleven must also be white. Even these eleven representatives are not secure; the Government, in pursuance of its policy of establishing local authorities in the Native Reserves, will probably abolish the seven Native Representatives altogether, and the desire to do so has already been expressed in high quarters.

One could be allowed to wonder if even the four Coloured Representatives would be safe. If *apartheid* for Coloured people makes any progress, they may one day have their own local authorities; they already have their own Coloured Affairs Department. Furthermore, many white South Africans find it intolerable to think that four Coloured Representatives might hold the balance of power in the Lower House. It must therefore be considered possible that one day the South African Parliament will consist only of white legislators who represent only white people. That is the trend, if not the goal, of contemporary politics.

►◄

However, a great number of white South Africans realize that this is an unstable position. The two major parties offer to stabilize it in different ways. Let us consider briefly their policies.

At least two policies are adopted by Afrikaner Nationalists. The Nationalists proceed on the assumption that it is totally and forever unthinkable that white and non-white people should live on equal terms within the same society; they therefore waver between two policies. The first is called Separate Development, i.e. granting equality by means of total territorial separation; this policy commends itself to idealists and intellectuals. The second is called *baasskap*, and means plainly White Supremacy; its supporters regard total territorial separation as impossible, and consider that 'white civilization' will survive only if one is prepared to fight for it. At the same time, a large number of Nationalists are able to justify the repressive laws of *baasskap*, because they regard them as steps towards total separation, which some authorities suppose to be a goal that may not be reached for a hundred or more years. Many Nationalists are thus able to live in two worlds, swallowing injustice in the one that is here, so that there may be justice in the other that is yet to come. It is what Professor B. B. Keet calls the 'pipe-dream'; and it has one striking characteristic, in that the more impossible the realization, the more insistently the dream is called up.

The second great party is the United Party, which on April 16, 1958, secured half of the votes of the country, and only one third of the seats. This Party represents the great majority of the English-speaking people and a hard but dwindling core of Afrikaners who inherit the old Botha-Smuts tradition of co-operation and reconciliation. This Party may also be said to have two ultimately irreconcilable policies, which are, however, combined in one, under the fine-sounding title, Discrimination with Justice. It is a city party, a more sophisticated party, and it believes in *ad hoc* decisions; it believes in a 'realistic' acceptance of present inevitabilities, and a 'progressive' adaptation to new events. Its leaders are therefore able to promise imaginative leadership to the continent of Africa, while having no political or social links with Africans at home. The Party is crippled by the necessity to conceal its *ad hoc* nature from those who want racial blueprints, and by the necessity to appear liberal in the eyes of the world and conservative in the eyes of the rural voter.

A small party which disappeared at the 1958 election was the Labour Party. Its two courageous and progressive M.P.s, Mr. Alex Hepple in Rosettenville and Mr. Leo Lovell in Benoni, having decided not to join the United Party, were crushed by it. The votes polled (Hepple 974, Lovell 1696) reveal two important truths; first, the United Party voter is not a supporter of progressive ideas; second, the number of progressive white voters is small. Compare the Hepple and Lovell totals with Brown (Liberal, Pietermaritzburg District, 604), Dey (Liberal, Orange Grove, 688), Gordon (Liberal, Sea Point, 1,642), in constituencies with approximately 11,000 voters. But another fact must be remembered; this was the first time since Union (1910) that liberal and progressive ideas had ever been put before the electorate. Meanwhile the Labour Party has disappeared. This was inevitable; it was an all-white party, and labour is nearly all black.

While the Labour Party has disappeared, the Liberal Party has just appeared. Today it is the party least affected by the sweeping election success of the Nationalists. It did not expect any improvement in the situation. It regards Nationalism and Liberalism as the real issue before the white voter. It did not expect any notable support from the electorate, because it stands for a common society with opportunity open to all, a goal unacceptable at present to most white South Africans, who have one great fear, namely that the white man will be swamped or even ejected.

Will the goal ever be acceptable? Is white South Africa preparing itself to enter the Nationalist fortress, where the struggle will be fought out, and to the death? Is there any hope for Liberalism, for a common society open to all, guaranteeing individual liberty and the rule of law, or will we exchange the rule of white nationalism for the rule of black nationalism? Even if that did happen, would it not still be necessary to champion liberal beliefs? Will black nationalism be animated by a desire for revenge? Or will black nationalism, because it has no fear of being 'swamped', be juster to white people than white nationalism was to black people? Finally, is 'change of heart' a quite non-political concept, with no political relevance; because we must face the fact that the Liberal Party of South Africa works for a 'change of heart', on both moral and practical grounds.

These are the questions that this little book will attempt to examine.

CHAPTER II

THE MEANING OF 'LIBERAL' IN SOUTH AFRICA

IT would first be wise to indicate the special meaning attaching to the words 'liberal' and 'liberalism' in South Africa. Liberalism in South Africa, though it has common elements with liberalism in other countries, and though its roots are the roots of liberalism everywhere, has nevertheless one characteristic which is especially its own, and that is its particular concern with racial justice. It is liberal in South Africa to want educated Africans to have a parliamentary vote; it is more liberal to want them to be able to stand for Parliament; it is even more liberal to want all Africans to participate fully in the processes of government.

It is liberal to want Indian traders to be allowed to trade in the central portion of a town or city and it is liberal to concern oneself with any injustice done to a non-white person. In the first half of last century it was liberal to want to protect slaves and servants from the punishments of harsh masters.

So the word 'liberal' in South Africa has come to have its own special meaning. It is possible to use it in other ways, including ways more readily understood in other countries, but in South Africa such a departure would need a word of explanation.

The word 'liberal' used by a liberal himself has, of course, a complimentary meaning. It may mean nothing more than that one is a white person who is in favour of the lifting of restrictions on non-white people, who is not bound hand and foot by racial custom and tradition and who is prepared to concede, not only a just ideal, but an increasing measure of just practice. In general, white members of the Liberal Party are more prepared for change than liberals outside it; in general they uphold equality of opportunity and of status as between white and non-white people, though some would insist on a transitional period towards such equality and others would proclaim it tomorrow if they could.

But there are other liberals who are not white persons. They are therefore upholding more than the right of non-white people to equality with white people. They are upholding the rights of all people and are defending what have been recognized as man's fundamental freedoms, as against law or police or Parliament or State. Their presence in a Liberal organization is of inestimable value, because their liberalism springs from a different experience of life and therefore enriches the whole. Liberalism, therefore, as seen from either of these points of view, is the champion of individual man; it is on the alert to defend him from any encroachment on his freedom and his rights, it is desirous of creating a society in which life may be said to be human.

Further, the word 'liberal' has for the white enemies of South African Liberalism another meaning; it shares this further meaning with the words 'liberalist' and 'liberalistic'. This meaning is derogatory and carries the stigma of 'loose', 'careless', 'promiscuous'. A 'liberalist' may for some be merely a person who espouses a wrong-headed philosophy, but for others he will be a person who has lost his 'own-ness', who in being all things to all men has himself become nothing, who has lost kind and class and identity, who has sunk himself in a quicksand of shiftingness, who has no longer any pride in being the special man that God intended him to be, or in possessing the special language or in having the special culture that God intended him to have, and, what is more, to preserve, maintain and die for.

Therefore in South Africa white religious men and women can easily bring themselves to hate and despise liberalism, and to see it not as the espousal of racial justice, but rather as the philosophy of decadence, of people who, instead of protecting their 'ownness' as God intended, have chosen the easy way of indiscriminate mixing. It is therefore to be expected that many white enemies of liberalism should accuse liberals of careless lives, of sexual promiscuity, or of a tendency towards it, and in particular a sexual disregard for race and colour. It is also to be expected that these accusations against liberals are in the main hurled at them by the poorest and least educated of their white opponents.*

This 'carelessness' of liberals is supposed also to apply to matters of religion. Because a person is 'liberal' in religious matters, because he may know and like persons of other religions or of no religion, he is assumed to be atheist or agnostic or wholly indifferent; but if he is clearly religious, then he has clearly become obsessed by the 'love' of God, and has overlooked His majesty, His laws, His ordered creation, His decree of 'own-sort-ness'.

Further, in the sphere of religion, the liberal, because of his being all things to all men, has deserted dogma and fixedness and has become vaguely benevolent, and possibly finally a 'mere' humanist. It was for this reason that the

---

*When white students of Natal University picketed a Nationalist Party meeting and displayed placards protesting against University *Apartheid*, they were angrily shouted at, and exhorted in this public place to 'go and sleep with your kaffir girls'. Others of us have had similar experiences.

Dutch Reformed Church of South Africa, seeking ministers
for the new congregations formed by the Great Trek, turned
from Holland in dismay and finally chose their men from
the Free Church of Scotland.

The word 'liberal' has a further meaning which is given to
it by its more radical enemies, and in general this unfavour-
able meaning is attached to white liberals, others being
regarded as fools and dupes. To be 'liberal' is to these critics
to be weak and spineless and compromising, or to be
unwilling to make any real sacrifice for these noble ideals,
or to be unwilling to face the hard and bitter future of hard
and bitter conflict (and therefore to be unprepared for it),
or to be hypocrites who are concerned not with justice but
only with their own skins, or to be knowingly or un-
knowingly trying to blunt the edge of black resistance by
drawing off fighters into the pavilions of love.

This essay will attempt to make clear to the reader the
historical reasons for the particular meanings that the
word 'liberal' and its derivatives have acquired in South
Africa. It will attempt to give a brief history of South Africa,
without which it seems impossible to understand the
contemporary scene. It will attempt from a liberal point of
view to examine the present, and even to peer into the future.
It will examine the position, the function, the achievement,
the future of liberalism of the South African kind, and the
considerable challenges that confront it. While not neglect-
ing the contributions of unattached or non-political liberals,
and while endeavouring to present their view-point clearly,
the whole essay will be written from the standpoint of one
who is identified with the Liberal Party, and who thinks
that the Party best represents the liberal cause.

CHAPTER III

THE COMING OF THE DUTCH

A BRIEF history of South Africa, especially when written by one who is not an historian, may be subject to much criticism. There is, however, no other course to be taken. We cannot dispense with a history, and it must be brief.

I suppose it is true of all countries that it is impossible to grasp fully their politics unless one knows their histories. It is I think more true of South Africa than of most; for otherwise it is difficult to understand the cold but never dangerous relationship between English- and Afrikaans-speaking South Africans, or to understand the strange compound of fear, disgust, duty, justice and charity that is the attitude of the white South African to the non-white and the deep distrust that characterizes the non-white attitude towards the whites.

Nevertheless I shall at the outset apologize for my brief historical account, which has necessarily sacrificed detail for clarity. But at the same time I shall defend it, for I find it reasonably satisfactory under all the circumstances.

►◄

Herodotus, famed historian of antiquity, relates how Necho of Egypt, six hundred years before Christ, sen explorers down the east coast of Africa, with instructions to circumnavigate the continent and to return by way of the Mediterranean. This they did, returning to Egypt after an absence of three years. We suppose that these mariners saw Table Mountain from the sea, and that they were the first men to do so.

It was 2000 years later, in A.D. 1486, that the Cape was 'discovered'. In that year Bartholomew Diaz, sailing for King John of Portugal, got as far as Algoa Bay (Port Elizabeth), and apparently on his return voyage saw the Cape, which, according to some, he called the Cape of Storms; but King John, believing that the route to India was within grasp, renamed it the Cape of Good Hope. He was justified, because in 1497 Vasco da Gama passed beyond the Cape, named Natal, visited Mozambique and reached India.

In 1503 Antonio de Saldanha actually entered Table Bay, and for all we know his was the first ship ever to lie under the great mountain. He was almost certainly the first white man to climb it, and it was he who gave it the name of Table Mountain.

In 1580 Sir Francis Drake rounded the Cape, and called it 'the fairest Cape in the whole circumference of the earth'. In 1620 Captains Shilling and Fitzherbert annexed the Cape for King James, but the King refused to endorse their action.

Meanwhile the power of Portugal had declined, and in 1602 the great Dutch East India Company was established to trade with India and the Orient. So it happened that in 1652 the Company found it necessary to establish a refreshment station at the Cape, where green vegetables could be grown as a means of fighting the dreadful plague of scurvy, where the sick could be left for attention and where outgoing sailors could leave letters to be taken back to Holland by the next home-going ship.

The indigenous inhabitants of the Cape were not numerous. They were the Hottentots and the Bushmen. The Hottentots were a primitive pastoral people; some of them were drawn into the life of the new settlement, either as servants or as suppliers of cattle to the passing ships, while some of them retreated from these powerful intruders, north and north-east into the interior. The Bushmen were an even more primitive people; they were diminutive in stature, they were notable hunters with poisoned arrows and they have left behind fascinating rock paintings in caves. When they could not get meat, they lived on wild fruits, insects and roots. To them the cattle of other men were only another kind of game, and as they had raided the Hottentots in the past, now they raided the white man's herds and other possessions. The white man's civilization was so alien to them that they made no attempt whatever to come to terms with it, and so, harried and killed in consequence of their raids, they withdrew farther and farther into the caves of the mountains. As the white man advanced, they retreated still further, into the deserts; today few of them are left and they live in the Kalahari, where they are protected by the British Government in much the same way as animals are protected in the Kruger Park.

It was not the original intention of the Dutch East India Company that the new settlement should become a colony. Nevertheless it did not find company farming very successful, and in 1657 it allowed nine burghers to go farming on their own at Rondebosch, but placed them under many irksome restrictions. In fact the burghers grew more and more impatient of the rule of the Company and began to look upon it as an alien authority, with interests different from, and in some cases incompatible with, their own. As the burghers moved further and further from Cape Town, this incompatibility grew more marked, and it became a recurrent factor in subsequent history.

The Company offered such low prices for farm produce that in 1658, in an attempt to lower the costs of production, the first Negro slaves were imported from West Africa. Thereafter slaves were imported from Malaya also. In the Cape, slavery took a relatively mild form, and there do not survive in South Africa the terrible stories known in so many other countries. It was with these slaves that those Hottentots who stayed in the Cape gradually merged, thus producing, with the co-operation of white settlers and sailors, a separate people called the Cape Coloured people, who today number one and a third millions and speak the same language as the Afrikaner people. In the early beginnings, this separation of the Coloured from the white was anything but hard and fast; van Riebeeck promoted van Meerhof to the rank of surgeon just after he had married Eva, a Hottentot woman. But customs changed; as society became more settled, such marriages became less and less acceptable, and the white and coloured groups grew more and more separate. It is hardly necessary to say that as this colour division grew more and more discriminatory, many families who were in fact of mixed blood stoutly clung to their membership of the white group; it was also quite common for a light-skinned coloured person to 'pass', often with the help of his or her relatives.

The white people of the Cape grew slowly in numbers, and were strengthened by accessions of German and French immigrants, these latter the celebrated Huguenots, who brought new skill to a very raw wine industry. Many of them were settled on farms twenty, thirty miles from Cape

Town. The most adventurous settlers, however, became pastoralists rather than agriculturists, and moved further and further away, until finally they reached the wastes of the Karroo. They were, as we know, already impatient of the rule of the Company, and they lived in greater and greater isolation from the influences of Europe. Their Dutch language changed too, becoming much simplified, and adding to itself a host of new idioms influenced by the kind of country they lived in and the kind of life they led, by the ox, by the wagon, by the loneliness, by the dry watercourse and the thorn. This country and this life were as unlike Holland and its ways as any country and life could be, and the language had to find new words for new things and new experiences, and to give new meanings to old words. The language was at first simply called *die taal* or 'the language', but today it is called Afrikaans. The people were called at first the Afrikanders, today simply the Afrikaners, *people of Africa*. No word could show more clearly the way in which Europe had ceased to count for these pioneers.

No visitor to South Africa should fail to see the Karroo if he wishes to understand an important chapter in the genesis of the Afrikaner people. It is a hard country, encouraging what are sometimes called the masculine qualities, of courage, tenacity, inflexibility, discouraging the feminine qualities of gentleness, kindliness and compassion, so that even the traditional Afrikaner mother is first and foremost the fierce protectress of the nation and its honour.

The expansion over the Karroo was rapid. Smallpox had almost annihilated the Hottentots, and there was little to stop the advance of the trekker, or the *trekboer*, as he was called, or even more simply, the *boer*. The word *boer* means farmer, and the word *trekboer* means a farmer who treks about, looking for grazing. The Company tried to control this migration, but was not successful; and this hard, free life made the trekkers independent and impatient of control.

There was noticeable, even at this early time, a cleavage between the trekkers and the city people of Cape Town, the first a people of Africa, the second still largely a people of Europe. This cleavage was rendered more pronounced by the Great Trek of 1836, so that up till today we speak of a difference between the Afrikaner traditions of the Cape and the Transvaal. By this we mean, amongst other things, that the Transvaal attitude towards racial questions is harder and more uncompromising, two characteristic features, as we have noted, of the scenery of the Karroo. We may also note that the healing of this Afrikaner cleavage was due in large measure to the later acts of men like Rhodes and Milner; of all the creators of Afrikaner unity, these two were the greatest.

These conditions of isolation and wildness might well have led to degeneration, and did in some cases; but religion exercised a powerful influence over the people. Although the Church, like the Company, found it difficult to keep in touch with the trekkers, the Bible was their constant companion, and daily scripture reading with prayers was a feature of family life. In particular were the trekkers attracted by the stories of the patriarchs, which seemed most relevant to their hard and lonely life. And who could have been nearer to the patriarchs than they themselves, as they moved in the wilderness with their flocks and herds, with their menservants and their maidservants, amongst wild men and wild beasts, with no protection but their rifles and their God? One might be forgiven for supposing that the Old Testament seemed far more relevant than the New to their frontier life, and that the God of Israel was more comprehensible than the Lover of all mankind.

As for the land itself, with its space and freedom, with its oases of greenness and coolness amid the heat and rock and thorn, to it they gave a fierce and possessive love. How far indeed were they from Europe, and how far in this Karroo from the thousand waterways of Holland! This horse, this saddle, this rifle, this antelope running, this everlasting plain, this everlasting sun—this was life, yet you would find not one hint of it in all the picture galleries of Amsterdam.

About 1770 there were over 10,000 white people at the Cape, and about an equal number of slaves. Nine-tenths of these white people were burghers and about half of them lived in Cape Town and in the beautiful valleys beyond the Cape Flats. The other half were the trekboers of whom we have already spoken. Before their advance the Bushmen and the Hottentots had wasted away; but now they began to encounter a new contestant, the Bantu tribes slowly moving south, largely in the country below the great escarpment that shut off the interior of the subcontinent. This encounter was one of the supreme events in the history of the Afrikaner. In 1778 Governor van Plettenberg, after consulting some petty Xosa chieftains, tried to circumvent it by declaring the Fish River to be the boundary of northward expansion. But this arrangement, like every similar arrangement made subsequently, failed, partly because there was no black centralized government with which to deal, partly because both Boer and Xosa were cattle-owners, and were hungry for land. The Xosas, though without written language and technological skill, were fierce warriors of assegai and shield, with a rich language and a notable system of law and custom. It is believed that they arrived in what is today known as the Eastern Cape Province in the late 1500's, and that they would have reached the Cape of Good Hope in due course, had they not now encountered the Boers.

Van Plettenberg's frontier remained unfortified and restless; remote control was now quite beyond the powers of a failing Company and a declining Netherlands. Individuals crossed the Fish River, either to steal cattle or retrieve them, to barter or to work or to hunt. One person's act could easily involve all. There was incessant trouble, raiding, thefts, reprisals. Sometimes it happened that a farmer would return home from a journey to find that his whole family had been killed, his home burned and his animals stolen. Grim pictures of these events are still to be found on the walls of some Afrikaner homes, keeping alive memories of the days when white and black were bitter—and pitiless—enemies. The situation had got out of hand; the Boers drove *Landdrost* (Magistrate) Maynier out of his drostdy, because he was too much of a stickler for the rule of law. In 1795 the Boers of Graaff Reinet set up their own republic, followed four days later by the Boers of Swellendam. The whole border was in a state of chaos, and less and less did the trekboers look for salvation anywhere but in themselves.

So it was that the struggle to survive on a dangerous continent became the main thought of the trekboer's mind, the main purpose of the trekboer's life. Like the thorn tree, which was to play a large part as a poetic symbol in his literature a century later, he put his roots down into the rock and stone, and in the face of all calamity survived. His enmity with the black man was bitter and relentless, as was the black man's enmity with him. Between white men and black men, and more still between white men and black women, there could be no relationship except those of

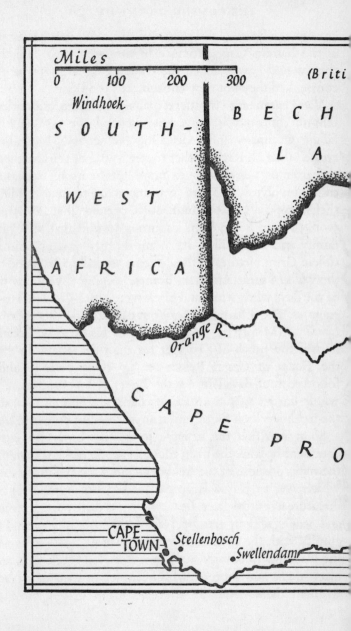

master and servant, or of enemy and enemy. The boer could only survive by keeping himself apart; only in *apartheid* was there any hope for the future of himself, his children and his race. What was more, his command of a written language, his superior technological skill, his possession of things like guns and wagons and, of course, the Bible, convinced him of the inferiority of his heathen foe.

And now, in September, 1795, the British occupied the Cape and inherited its frontier troubles. By now there were about 16,000 white people in the Colony and about 17,000 slaves. Graaff Reinet and Swellendam reluctantly submitted to the new government, not expecting to like it any better than the old. The British commander forbade the Boers to cross the boundaries. So began the turbulent nineteenth century, which General Smuts was to call the Century of Wrong.

CHAPTER IV

THE COMING OF THE BRITISH

THE coming of the British to the Cape in 1795 (and finally in 1806), was the second supreme event of Afrikaner history. It was the British who scattered these widely dispersed elements still more widely over the subcontinent, and who finally welded them all together again. This is not to deny the Afrikaners' own part in their making, but to emphasize the part of the British as external agent.

It has been said that Afrikanerdom could not exist without its enemies, and that these are two in number, namely the British and the Bantu. This generalization has all the defects of its kind, but conveys a real truth. English-speaking South Africans are sometimes startled by the speeches of Afrikaner politicians, who bring out the skeleton of British Imperialism and set its bones a-jangling, which has the effect of simultaneously chilling and heating the electoral blood. But there are signs that the skeleton is losing its power, and that its place is now being taken by other external enemies, for example, world opinion, United Nations, Communism, Mr. Nehru, the new American imperialism, British negrophiles and, nearer home, the English press and the Anglican Church. It is a characteristic of Afrikaner nationalism that it needs these enemies, even while it wistfully wishes it did not. This ambivalence is strikingly displayed in the government's attitude towards Ghana, where genuine pleasure over Ghana's independence is adulterated by the realization that the Ghanaian is the blood-brother of the enemy at home. Thus we have the ridiculous, or rather pathetic, spectacle of a black Ghanaian visitor enjoying a hospitality and an immunity in South Africa that has never yet been accorded to any black citizen of the Union.

►◄

The arrival of the British at the Cape was followed by a great expansion of missionary activity. As might be expected, the attitude of the missionaries to the Hottentots and the Xosas was not the same as that of the farmers; to the missionaries these indigenous people were souls to be saved, to the farmer they were labourers in whose education and social advance he was not much interested, though he sometimes took an interest in their spiritual welfare.

The attitude of the British administrators, though by no means identical with that of the missionaries, was nevertheless different from that of the colonists. While nothing was done in the beginning to weaken the rights of slave-owners, yet the rights of both slaves and servants to good treatment was confirmed, and the courts were ordered to see that such treatment was given. One of the earliest results of this order was the famous Black Circuit of 1811, where many a white farmer had to face charges of ill-treatment, preferred against him as a result of complaints from a coloured man. One may say that two new ideas entered the Cape at this time; or alternatively that two old ideas were suddenly remembered, namely the equality of all men before God, and the equality of all men before the law.

So officials, colonists and missionaries lived in an uneasy triangular relationship. The officials had to consider the difficulties of the farmers, but they had to consider also the powerful support in England for the missionaries. These missionaries sent back reports to England, some of them hostile to the colonists.

Equally were the colonists hostile to the missionaries. Hottentots flocked to the mission stations, where they found conditions easier than on the farms. The farmers, as is always the case in South Africa, were short of labour, and regarded the religious zeal of the Hottentots as so much pretence, which no doubt it often was. They were angered also by the acts of missionary Vanderkemp who, himself no longer young, married a Hottentot girl whose sole possessions were two sheepskins and some beads. Times had changed since Eva married the surgeon van Meerhof with the approval of the Commander. By his marriage this newcomer, this *uitlander* (outlander), had affronted Afrikaner opinion; and, what is more, the colonist could see no point in educating non-white people for a life that simply did not exist and for which they would have been in any case unfitted in his view.

There is an important point to be noted here, and that is that most of the missionaries were British. This animus against the missionaries has persisted in South Africa to this very day, and was undoubtedly one of the chief motives behind the Bantu Education Act of 1954, which brought missionary education almost to an end and refused to allow famous institutions such as the century-old Adams College, Huddleston's St. Peter's in Rosettenville and the Methodist Kilnerton College to continue as private schools. But while these losses are being suffered, the missionary work of the Dutch Reformed Churches, once negligible, is expanding

23

rapidly; the Afrikaner Nationalist cannot really feel safe until even African religion is in his hands.

In 1815, under this new British rule, a Hottentot servant complained of the treatment he had received from his master, Frederick Bezuidenhout. Bezuidenhout treated the summons of the court with contempt, and a European officer with Hottentot soldiers was sent to arrest him. To send Hottentots to arrest a white man had never been done before. Bezuidenhout fought the party from a cave, but was killed. At his funeral his brother swore to avenge this outrage and he and his friends rebelled. The rebellion was soon put down, and five of the men were publicly hanged by Lord Charles Somerset at Slagter's Nek. It is not clearly known what the reaction of the farmers was to this grim event; but in later times the hanged men were looked upon as martyrs who had died for the cause of the Afrikaner against the British Government, the missionaries and the cursed doctrines of equality. Slagter's Nek is to this day remembered, one of the great and bitter events of the Century of Wrong.

In 1820 came the first large group of English-speaking colonists, about 5,000 in number. Most of the settlers came to the disturbed frontier area, and founded the towns of Port Elizabeth and Grahamstown. One result of their coming was to make the British Government attempt to anglicize the Afrikaner Dutch, and English took the place of Dutch as the official language. The Dutch landdrosts were replaced by magistrates, the Dutch rix-dollars by pounds, shillings and pence, and only English and Latin were taught in the state-aided schools. This attempt at anglicization angered the Afrikaner Dutch, and even today the name of the Governor, Lord Charles Somerset, is remembered with detestation.

Another important event of this period is the passage of the 50th Ordinance, which secured the civil rights of coloured people. This evidence of a further move towards equality also angered the farmers. They saw the weakening of authority over the Hottentots; they feared increased vagrancy and idleness, and further shortages of labour.

Then came another important event, the order for the emancipation of 800,000 slaves through the British Empire. For South African slaves worth £2,800,000 compensation of £1,250,000 was to be paid, and that in London. Speculators visited the farms and bought up the claims at a heavy discount.

Finally in 1834 there was the Sixth Kaffir War.* The Xosas poured across the frontier, burning, destroying and killing. The Governor, Sir Benjamin D'Urban, fixed a new frontier, the Kei River, which was another eighty miles farther north. He proclaimed the new province of Queen Adelaide, and offered protection to all. Just when the farmers, who were hungry for more land, were congratulating themselves on their new Governor, the British Government reversed his policy, brought the frontier back to the Fish River, and declared that 'the Kaffirs had an ample justification' for the war.

This was the last straw for the farmers. They had had enough of British government, British missionaries, British public opinion. The Hottentots had been granted unheard of rights, the slaves had been freed, black men were being treated like white men, their whole patriarchal world was

---

*The word 'kaffir' is the most offensive that any European can use of an African. It still lingers on in terms such as 'Kaffir Wars', which Africans prefer to call 'Frontier Wars'. It also lingers on, causing insoluble problems, in names such as 'kaffirboom', the beautiful flowering tree *Erythrina caffra*. A gardener may use this Latin name, or he may use the Zulu name, 'umsinsi', but very few people will know what he is talking about. Problem-conscious gardeners refer to it wryly as the 'African boom' or 'African tree'!

tumbling about their ears. So, party by party, beginning in 1836, they set out north on the Great Trek, climbing the mountains onto the great interior plain, crossing the Orange River into the grasslands, in the direction of Kimberley, Bloemfontein, Johannesburg, Pretoria, all yet unborn, crossing east over the Drakensberg into Natal where the missionary Gardiner had given the name of Durban to the little trading settlement at Port Natal. Among the many trekkers, computed to have been over 5,000 in number, was a young lad of ten, Paul Kruger, who sixty-three years later was to lead his Transvaal Republic against Britain in the Anglo-Boer War.

'We quit this Colony,' wrote Pieter Retief, one of the foremost Voortrekkers, 'under the full assurance that the English Government has nothing more to require of us, and will allow us to govern ourselves without its interference in future.' Retief's English neighbours (for the Border was a largely English-speaking area) saw him go with regret, and presented him with a Bible to take on his journey.

It will be seen that there were many causes for the Great Trek, one of them being undoubtedly the hunger for land, which had been causing expansion incessantly since 1652. The Great Trek, though it had spontaneous characteristics, had nevertheless been prepared for by preliminary journeys made by scouts into the far interior. But undoubtedly the deepest cause of the trek was the incompatibility of British Government with Afrikaner Boer, particularly in their respective views on the vexed matter of race and colour. Even today nothing is resented more by the Afrikaner, and indeed by most white South Africans, than to have their racial policies criticized by European or American; the critic is told that 'he has not lived in the country'. If this critic is an

Englishman, a missionary, an Anglican, his criticism is still more resented. At times this resentment will go so far as to extend itself to the English-speaking South African, who has not yet been 300 years in the country, though this argument has fallen into disuse since Dr. Verwoerd, Mr. Strijdom's lieutenant, came to his present position of almost dictatorial power, because Dr. Verwoerd was born in Europe, and was two years old when his father emigrated to South Africa.

A Voortrekker woman, Anna Steenkamp, sister of Pieter Retief, wrote what to my mind is the most important statement on the Great Trek. She wrote '. . . . the shameful and unjust proceedings with reference to the freeing of our slaves; and yet it is not so much their freeing which drove us to such lengths, as their being placed on an equal footing with Christians, contrary to the laws of God, and the natural distinctions of race and colour, so that it was intolerable for any decent Christian to bow down beneath such a yoke; wherefore we rather withdrew in order to preserve our doctrines in purity.'

Here was Pieter Retief, an upright and respected man, obviously one of substance and integrity, and not lacking in determination and courage. But to him the liberal idea of a common society to which both white and black might belong was unthinkable; what was more, it would remain unthinkable. For him, as for his sister, there were natural distinctions of race and colour. It might be said that for him race was an immutable category. *Apartheid* was therefore for him a morality, a religion, a philosophy, and a politics all in one. It is necessary to understand this if we are to understand present-day South Africa.

It was a courageous act on the part of the Voortrekkers, when they knew so well the fighting qualities of the African tribes, to go still farther into the interior. But two things favoured them; one was their superior technology, that is, their guns, the other was the state of chaos in the interior, owing to the fact that Shaka, the fighting King of the Zulus, had set tribe after tribe, and faction after faction, fleeing from him and from one another, in directions radiating from Zululand like the spokes of a wheel, affecting African life as far north as Nyasaland.

Shaka was succeeded by Dingaan, and when Retief had crossed over the escarpment of the Drakensberg into Natal, he left a few men and all the women and children encamped, and with sixty followers went to see the Zulu king in order to make a treaty. Retief and his whole party were slaughtered by the king, who promptly sent 10,000 warriors to the encampment and killed all who were there, at a place thereafter to be called Weenen, which name means weeping. The trekkers found a new leader in Andries Pretorius, after whom Pretoria was named. On December 16, 1838, after having vowed to God to keep the day holy if He would give them victory, Pretorius humbled Dingaan's armies at the battle of Blood River. It is said that three Boers were slightly wounded, but that 3,000 Zulus were slain.

Thus December 16 was called Dingaan's Day for more than a century, and only recently has its name been changed to the Day of the Covenant. It is religiously observed by many Afrikaners, but not by English-speaking South Africans, who, until prevented by a growing uneasiness (partly caused by the increasing power of Afrikaner Nationalism) and finally by law, used it to hold race-meetings and cricket matches. It is fair to say that the Day of the Covenant means little to the English-speaking South African, while to the African, the black man, it gives offence. And indeed this is not surprising, for the Day is often used by Afrikaner speakers to dwell on the bitter enmities of the past and the necessity for continuing them into the future. Nothing could show more clearly than the Day of the Covenant the terrible divisions of South Africa.

On December 16, 1938, one hundred years after the battle of Blood River, was laid the foundation stone of the great Voortrekker Monument, now standing on a commanding site on one of the Pretoria hills. The Monument was built to commemorate the struggle of Christianity against Barbarism, which means, to put it bluntly, the struggle of the Voortrekkers against the African people. This struggle is portrayed, by means of a magnificent frieze in Italian marble, in restrained and dignified fashion, but the shrine remains first and last an Afrikaner shrine, though it may be visited by non-white people on Tuesday afternoons. One here records with deep regret that this most sacred shrine of Afrikaner pride and piety evokes no more than a cold respect from anyone who is not an Afrikaner. The symbolic laager of wagons which surrounds the monument and was intended to shut out anything that is non-Afrikaner, succeeds only too well in its excluding purpose.

CHAPTER V

'THE CENTURY OF WRONG'

THE battle of Blood River was a decisive event. The interior of South Africa fell to the invader, even though only after a determined struggle. Moshesh managed to keep Basutoland free, but in 1864 he put his country under the protection of the Queen. In 1885 Bechuanaland came under the same protection, but the position of Swaziland remained ambiguous until 1903, when it too became a country protected by Britain. These are the three countries often referred to as the protectorates, which the South African Government has consistently wished to incorporate in the Union; but up till now Britain has consistently refused her consent. She is in fact shortly to introduce a modified form of responsible government in Basutoland.

Meanwhile in 1853 the Cape Colony was granted representative government, and a non-racial franchise. In 1852, by the Sand River Convention, Britain assured the Transvaalers that she would no longer concern herself with their affairs, and in 1854, by the Bloemfontein Convention, she gave the Orange Free State a similar assurance. It is significant that the South African Republic (not the only independent Transvaal state at that time) was based on a constitution that declared 'no equality in church or state'.

The Voortrekkers also established the Republic of Natal in 1838, but it was short-lived. British traders and missionaries had been active at Durban Bay and along the Natal coast since 1824, and had actually obtained a grant of land from the Zulu king Shaka before he was murdered by Dingaan. However, the British Government made no move to recognize this settlement until the Boer Republic, in 1841, sent a punitive expedition to the south against the Bacas, who had stolen some cattle. Still further south, the Pondos, fearing worse to come, appealed to the Cape Government, whereupon the British annexed Natal. The boers besieged the British in Durban and Dick King made his famous ride of 600 miles to Grahamstown in ten days, through a wild and unknown country, to ask for reinforcements. As a result of these events most of the Voortrekkers trekked back over the escarpment, and Natal, as a result of immigration, became the largely English-speaking province that it is today, if we consider only its white inhabitants. Otherwise considered, it was, and still is, predominantly Zulu-speaking.

Dick King is today a hero, and his statue stands on the Esplanade in Durban. Some English-speaking people, envious of the Afrikaans periodical re-enactments of historic events, would like to see the famous ride re-enacted every May 25. But the truth is that English-speaking people are not capable of emulating the Afrikaner's commemorative fervour.

In 1856 Natal became a British Crown Colony, also initially with a franchise not based on colour. In Natal, the Transvaal and the Orange Free State, the white man, by virtue of his armaments, subdued the tribesmen; he allowed many of them to settle on his farms, for the others he created areas called Reserves. Today in South Africa these Reserves constitute about 13% of the total land area, while the African people constitute about 66% of the total population. This remains one of their deep grievances, healed to some extent by urbanisation, but breaking out again now that the policy of the government is to regard the Reserves as the home of the African, and to regard the town-dweller as a 'temporary sojourner' in the white man's territory.

It is today claimed that the reserve policy was motivated by the loftiest feelings. But it will do us no harm to recognize it as a policy of conquer, divide and rule, offering to the conquered a restricted life in a restricted area, encouraging him to come out of his Reserve to work, and subjecting him in the city to a host of restrictive regulations, some of which are quite pitiless in their operation. In the towns and villages the African people live in locations, their entry and departure are controlled, and the legislation which governs their lives is open to manifold abuses. It is only in recent years that the conscience of white South Africa has become increasingly troubled by the squalor of the locations, and more has been done to improve the material conditions under the present Nationalist Government than under any other. But the vicious laws remain.*

On the whole, relations between the British and the Boers began to improve after the Great Trek, and they might have gone on improving if a trader called O'Reilly had not seen the 'pretty Orange River stone' at the home of Mr. van Niekerk in 1866, in the dry country near Kimberley.

*An African boy, living with his family in a location, may on attaining the age of 16 be ordered by the Location Superintendent to return to the place of his birth

The Boer republic of the Orange Free State claimed this area, under the Bloemfontein Convention of 1854, by which the British guaranteed the independence of the country between the Orange and the Vaal. But a Griqua chief named Waterboer also claimed the area, and when he applied to the British for protection they annexed his territory. In 1876, in the light of further evidence, the British Government paid the Orange Free State an amount of £90,000 in compensation, but the damage had been done.

Meanwhile the other Boer republic, the Transvaal, almost bankrupt, was seriously threatened by disturbances in the large reserve of Sekhukhuneland. With this as reason, but no doubt with the further intention of achieving the unification of South Africa under the Union Jack, the British annexed the Transvaal in 1877. This not only further antagonised the two republics, but also many Afrikaners who had remained behind in the Cape Colony. Slowly but surely the British Government was uniting such opinion throughout South Africa; it was about this time indeed that the unifying name of Afrikaner, as distinct from Transvaaler, Free Stater and Cape Colonial, began to come more and more into use. It began to appear to the Boers that the British Empire, despite the Conventions of Bloemfontein and Sand River, was intent on swallowing up the Republics; so that what had been an anti-Government feeling began to change into something more specifically anti-British.

In 1880 the Transvaal Burghers rose; the British suffered a severe defeat at Majuba, which is another event that remains forever green in Afrikaner memory. In 1881 the war ended without victory; self-government was restored to the Transvaal, but in foreign affairs it was to be subject to the Queen's suzerainty. There was however a strong sentiment for complete independence, and Paul Kruger, who became President in 1883, became the embodiment of it.

The next great event to hit South Africa was the discovery of gold on the Witwatersrand in 1886. Cecil Rhodes already controlled the Diamond Fields; he was now a millionaire and had great dreams of an all-British route from the Cape to Cairo and of the unification of South Africa under the Union Jack. But Kruger stood in his way; therefore Rhodes sought to contain and confine the Transvaal Republic. He became Prime Minister of the Cape Colony, acquired the territory of British Bechuanaland (which is not to be confused with Bechuanaland Protectorate) and established the new country of Rhodesia. So, with Mozambique to the east and Natal to the south, Kruger was contained.

Then Rhodes turned his attention to the Witwatersrand itself, where he already had great financial interests. Into Johannesburg had poured thousands of immigrants, called the uitlanders by the outnumbered Boers. Kruger altered the voting qualifications to prevent the immigrants from securing control. There was great dissatisfaction, and Rhodes meant to use it. In 1895 his friend Jameson, having failed to receive an urgent message ordering him to desist, entered the Transvaal with 500 armed men in the famous Jameson Raid. The hoped-for rising of the uitlanders failed to come off, the British Government repudiated the raiders, and Jameson had to surrender ignominiously to Cronje. Kruger, against the advice of some of his more stubborn commandants, handed the whole party over to the British authorities for punishment.

That was the end of the influence of Cecil Rhodes in South Africa. He was a great man with great ideas; he controlled Kimberley at 27, built great houses, became a Prime Minister, gave his name to a country, founded the most famous scholarships in history and chose for himself one of the grandest burial places in the world. He expected to be remembered for 4,000 years, but, except on ceremonial occasions in Rhodesia, he is remembered chiefly for the incalculable harm that he did to Anglo-Afrikaner relations.

Kruger, encouraged by the failure of the raid, now took a stronger line with the uitlanders. But the British Government sent out as High Commissioner an opponent harder and colder than Rhodes, namely Alfred (later Lord) Milner. That he must bear the major blame for the Anglo-Boer War is clear from his papers, which are published for all to read.

In October, 1899, the Republics declared war on Britain. It was called a 'gentleman's war' and was generally free of brutality and atrocity. The British command pursued a 'scorched earth' policy; it burned the farms and put the women and children into concentration camps, where over 20,000 of them died, mostly because of insanitary conditions that were improved when the rising number of deaths shocked the military into action. This is another of the tragic events of the Century of Wrong that is freshly remembered, that seems never likely to be forgotten, that even today is argued about by correspondents to the newspapers, in angry and bitter terms.

The war could end in only one way, and on May 31, 1902, the Treaty of Vereeniging was signed. The two republics of the Orange Free State and the Transvaal became British colonies, the former now being known as the Orange River Colony. The unification of the four British colonies was thus brought nearer, but its two white races had never been further apart.

CHAPTER VI

THE RISE OF THE AFRIKANER

AFTER the Anglo-Boer War, there was a period of energetic reconstruction in which the Governor of the two new colonies, Lord Milner, played an outstanding and admirable part. But he was an autocrat, and entertained the foolish plan of anglicizing the Boer population. Luckily there were great-minded men in Britain and South Africa at this time. In 1905 Campbell-Bannerman and the Liberal Party came into power in Britain, and in 1906 restored self-government to the Transvaal, and in 1907 to the Orange River Colony. The first Prime Minister of the Transvaal was the Boer General Louis Botha, with the Boer General Smuts as Secretary of State. The first Prime Minister of the Orange River Colony was Mr. Abraham Fischer, with the Boer General Hertzog as his Attorney-General. English was to be the official language, but Dutch could be freely used in debates. The vote was limited to European adult males in these two colonies.

The importance of these events could hardly be overestimated. They marked the end of British Imperialism. They marked the approaching end of the colonial age and the beginning of an age of liberation and turbulence which has by no means reached its end.

In 1910 all four colonies formed the Union of South

Africa, and its first Prime Minister was General Louis Botha. Racial conciliation was in the air. The English and Dutch languages were declared equal. A wave of goodwill spread over the country. The Cape of Good Hope, which in 1853 had achieved self-government, had a non-racial franchise and several thousands of Cape Coloured and African voters; this franchise was to be preserved, but not to be extended to the other three provinces of the Union. Further, it could only be altered by a two-thirds majority of both Houses sitting together. These conditions were not secured, as many Afrikaner Nationalists suppose today, by the intervention of the British Government, but by representatives of the Cape Colony itself. All four colonies agreed, however, that whatever the voting rights of non-white people, no non-white person might be elected to either House of Parliament. And lastly, on the insistence of the rural areas of the Cape and Free State, it was agreed that a rural constituency might be underloaded up to 15%, and an urban one overloaded up to 15%. This had far-reaching consequences in later years.

But although there was much talk of brotherhood and reconciliation between the white races, there were large numbers of Afrikaner Nationalists who would have nothing to do with it. They were too near to the events of the Century of Wrong. They welcomed the recognition of Dutch, but they wanted rather the recognition of Afrikaans. Jealously they guarded everything that was peculiar to themselves, knowing the dangers of an alien culture; for were there not Afrikaners in the Cape who had become more English than the English? Above all, they insisted that their children should be educated in Afrikaans-medium schools, and for their young men and women they established Afrikaans-medium universities.

Afrikaner Nationalism worked openly and boldly for

political supremacy. After all, Afrikaners outnumbered English-speaking South Africans, and if only they could be made Nationalists, if only they would use properly the franchise now restored to them, if only they would rebuild their own and not be misled by soft words, then one day they would not only win back the old Republics, but would establish the new Republic of South Africa. Then would Afrikanerdom be triumphant, and South Africa would truly belong to those who had suffered for her so greatly.

The Nationalists now set out to accomplish this task. In 1912 General Hertzog broke away from General Botha, and formed the small Nationalist Party. In 1914 came the First World War, and General Botha took South Africa into it at the side of Great Britain; but much of Afrikaans-speaking South Africa would have nothing to do with a 'British' war. Some rebelled; one named Jopie Fourie was shot as a traitor, and he, too, went to join the ranks of the martyrs of Slagter's Nek.

In 1924 the Nationalists under General Hertzog, aided by a small largely-English-speaking Labour Party, captured the Government. One of their first acts was to establish Afrikaans as equal with English. Another was to get away from the hated Union Jack, and to have a Union Flag; this was bitterly opposed by English-speaking South Africa, and the compromise is the flag we know today, the flag of Orange, with, superimposed on the middle bar, three small flags, replicas of the Union Jack and the two republican flags. Dr. Malan called this 'the scab' and said it would one day fall off. Another important event was when the British Parliament passed the Statute of Westminster in 1931, declaring the absolute equality of status of all Dominions within the British Commonwealth of Nations, which were inited only by their common allegiance to the Crown. South Africa thus became the equal of Great Britain and the mistress of her own destinies.

English-speaking South Africa, which, after Botha's death, had given almost full support to Smuts, was relieved when Hertzog and Smuts joined in 1933, in the United Party. But a small number of Nationalists again stood aloof, this time under Dr. Malan.

In 1936 Hertzog obtained the necessary two-thirds majority in a joint sitting for the transfer of all African voters to a separate roll. Eleven members out of 190 opposed the change, led by J. H. Hofmeyr. In 1938 'Die Stem van Suid-afrika' became a national anthem alongside of 'God Save the King'.

In 1939 came the Second World War. Hertzog and Smuts differed violently, but Smuts with a majority of thirteen votes again led South Africa into war at the side of Great Britain. Hertzog was reunited with Malan and the Nationalists, but soon after died. There was no rebellion; very many Afrikaners joined the forces, but on the whole the Dutch Reformed Churches, the Afrikaner cultural societies, the Afrikaans-medium schools, the Universities of Stellenbosch, Bloemfontein, Potchefstroom and Pretoria, stood quite aloof.

Smuts and his United Party came victoriously through the war, but were defeated by Malan and his Nationalists in 1948. This was the first all-Afrikaner Government in South Africa; it held the majority of seats, but owing to the underloading and overloading mentioned above, it did so by a minority of votes.

How did the Nationalists finally get in? Who put them in? There is no doubt that with a few exceptions they were put in by the Afrikaner people. There is no doubt that at no time in their long history had so many of the Afrikaners thought as one. After forty years of Union, during which there had been a minimum of brawling, public and private fighting and violence, the English-speaking and the Afrikaans-speaking South Africans had never been so divided.

And why did they get in? There is no doubt that they got in because they promised to solve the racial problems of the Union in the traditional Boer way, by the methods of separation or *apartheid*; that is, by separating the races in schools, universities, residential areas, occupations and professions, trains and buses, entrances and exits, libraries, halls, and in every other desirable way. At last the Afrikaner people had a chance to make good the wrong turning that history had taken when the British and their missionaries came to the Cape, and to re-assert the supremacy of the white man. In the words of the *Grondwet*, the Constitution, of the Transvaal Republic, there was to be 'no equality in Church or State'.

One of the cries of the 1948 election was that Hofmeyr must be destroyed. It was he who had opposed the transfer of African voters to a separate roll. It was he who had resisted Smuts' attempts to restrict Indians to certain areas. It was he who always insisted that the brotherhood of man must be translated into political terms. On December 3, 1948, he died, some said of a broken heart, rightly I think. No man in South Africa foresaw so clearly how ruthlessly the Nationalists would carry out their policy of *apartheid*.

The first year of office was relatively quiet. The recently granted Parliamentary representation for Indians was repealed. Immigration was curtailed, because immigrants had an unfortunate habit of siding with the United Party. Malan called the United Nations a 'menace to liberty' and threatened to leave the organization rather than subject the mandated territory of South-West Africa (the one-time German colony) to U.N. inspection. Malan's lieutenant, Strijdom, said that resistance to *apartheid* was treasonable. The Minister of Education cut down the grants for feeding African schoolchildren and the animus of the Government against inter-racial trade unions was clearly revealed.

In 1949 came the Mixed Marriages Act, and the Government closed twenty-one cities and towns to African work-seekers. In 1950 came the Population Registration Act, introducing a scheme of classification by which the race of all persons would be once and forever determined, a measure which was to cause unspeakable suffering, and to cause wives to repudiate husbands and children to hate fathers, because fear of ostracism was now great enough to overcome love of kindred. This Population Registration Act was essential to Acts like the Mixed Marriages Act, the Immorality Act, and especially now to the new Group Areas Act, which was to divide the whole Union into racial areas.

In presenting the Group Areas Bill to Parliament, Dr. Donges, Minister of the Interior, said that it would be implemented 'with justice to all'. One of the first effects of the Act has been to expel Indian traders in the Transvaal from the centres of all cities and towns; in Johannesburg the expulsion will be to the bare veld twenty miles from the city. Another effect has been to expel African owners from freehold sites, and to offer them other sites where they may not purchase land. In every declaration of group areas it is always the white group that is left alone; in the city of Durban it is estimated that 3,000 whites will be moved, and over 100,000 other persons. The Act further gave inspectors the right to enter any dwelling by day or by night, and without notice. The United Party supported this evil legislation, because while it believes in economic integration, it also believes in social and residential separation enforced by law.

Also in 1950 came the Suppression of Communism Act, under which the Minister might 'deem' any person to be a Communist, and compel him to resign from all societies and organizations, and forbid him to speak publicly or to enter certain areas. There is no appeal from any such ban. On Labour Day the African and Indian Congresses held a protest meeting on the Rand and lost eighteen killed in fighting with the police. The first South-West Africa elections, giving to white voters a representation three times as generous as in the Union, were a triumph for Malan, giving him four more Senators and six more M.P.s. On September 11, 1950, Smuts died; and Dr. Jansen having resigned to become Governor-General, Dr. Verwoerd was appointed Minister of Native Affairs. He was to be the Supreme Architect of *apartheid*.

In 1951 came the Bantu Authorities Act, which got rid of the troublesome Native Representative Council and began creating a hierarchy of authorities all under the Minister of Native Affairs. In the struggle to remove Coloured voters from the common roll, the Government, acting on the assumption that the Statute of Westminster freed the now autonomous Union of South Africa from any obligation to observe the entrenchments of the Constitution, voted the removal by an ordinary majority. The Minister of Education threatened the withholding of grants from cultural societies that did not observe the colour bar, and the Christian Education Movement, for one, decided to continue without State support. Passports were made Government property, and several hundreds of people were 'named' under the Suppression of Communism Act. The exciting event of the year was the formation of the Torch Commando; thousands of ex-servicemen and others marched on Cape Town and demonstrated against the removal of Coloured voters, and the Commando was at first able to conceal its typically White-South-Africa dilemma, namely that it was defending the rights of coloured people, but was not prepared to make common cause with them. The Commando went from strength to strength, the flush of fever disguising its fatal malady.

In 1952 Dr. Verwoerd introduced his Bantu Urban Authorities Act, whereby he hoped still further to divide and rule the African people. The Appellate Court invalidated the Separate Representation of Voters Act, whereupon the Government secured the passing of the High Court of Parliament Act, making Parliament an Appellate Court of higher status than the one in Bloemfontein. The exciting event of this year was the launching of the Resistance movement, and many thousands of non-white volunteers broke the *apartheid* laws, to be joined later by Patrick Duncan, son of the late Sir Patrick Duncan, first South African citizen to be appointed Governor-General, and other Europeans. The High Court of Parliament invalidated the Appellate invalidation, and the Cape Supreme Court invalidated the High Court invalidation, and was on appeal supported by the Appellate Court. The Resistance Movement was marred by ugly riots at Port Elizabeth and East London, in which Europeans were killed; the leaders disowned the rioters, but their resistance was believed by many people to have opened the door to lawless elements. The white Congress of Democrats was formed, a radical organization resolutely opposed to *apartheid* and destined to co-operate closely with the African and Indian Congresses. So came to an end a troubled year.

In 1953 Parliament passed the Public Safety Act, carried

with nine dissentients and supported by the United Party. The Criminal Law Amendment Act was passed to counteract the Resistance Movement, providing for penalties of £300 and/or three years and/or lashes for law-breaking by way of protest, and penalties of £500 and/or five years and/or lashes for incitement to protest. This brought the Resistance Movement to an end, and many of its leaders were banned, including ex-Chief Luthuli, President-General of the African National Congress.

In the General Elections the Nationalists secured nine more seats, though still with a minority of votes. This led to the formation of the Liberal Party to replace the Liberal Association; the Party observed no colour bar in membership and opposed all discriminatory laws. The Federal Party also came into being, declaring its opposition to a republic, and its support for a federal constitution, but taking no firm stand on the question of racial discrimination. But tragically the Torch Commando went into a decline. Parliament passed the Separate Amenities Act, which empowered authorities to maintain and set up facilities separate but not equal for the various races. Dr. Malan, the Prime Minister, tried again for a two-thirds majority to remove Coloured voters to a separate roll, but failed. The reservation of occupations to specific racial groups was foreshadowed, and Dr. Malan threatened those universities which admitted non-white students and again pressed the claim of South Africa to incorporate the Protectorates.

In 1954 Dr. Malan failed again to secure a two-thirds majority to remove the Coloured voters, being unable to persuade the United Party to support him. The dreaded Industrial Conciliation Act was passed, permitting no trade unions for Africans, no multi-racial unions, and allowing the Minister to allocate occupations on a racial basis. The forty-year-old freehold African suburb of Johannesburg called Sophiatown was declared a white area, and Dr. Verwoerd, having failed to secure the co-operation of the Johannesburg City Council, secured the passing of an Act to establish a Native Resettlement Board to remove the residents of Sophiatown to Meadowlands, where they would enjoy no freehold rights. This was done in pursuance of the theory that the African was a 'temperorary dweller' in the cities, and excited wonder in the minds of dispassionate observers that the Minister could so foolishly destroy an African land-owning class that would not be likely to lend itself to revolution or violence. Dr. Verwoerd also sponsored the Bantu Education Act, which meant the end of missionary activity in the field of education. The Minister said in the House that there was no place for Africans in the European community 'above the level of certain forms of labour'. Bantu schools were to be community schools, not under missionary control, but under the control of community committees, controlled not by the community, but by the Minister. Those schools which wished to continue as private schools must gain the consent of the Minister. The Dutch Reformed Churches approved the Act, as did some of the subservient foreign missions; but the other churches protested.

In December was held a Multi-racial Church Conference in Johannesburg, under the aegis of the Dutch Reformed Churches, in which speakers and delegates of all races took part, although they sat and ate separately. The United Party promised a new non-European policy, but its Congress produced virtually nothing; and the overwhelmingly English-speaking Natal Provincial Council forbade inter-racial sport at any of its educational institutions. Another gloomy year.

In 1955 Malan resigned, and Strijdom succeeded him. He saw the future as a struggle between Nationalism and Liberalism, but promised 'white supremacy with justice for all'. The Group Areas Act was further amended to speed up the proclamations, which were being delayed by the tactics of the Indian Congress, and the Group Areas Development Act was passed, which empowered the authorities, after hearing representations, to value properties, from which valuation there was no appeal.

On June 25 and 26, the Congress of the People was held at Kliptown. Three thousand delegates attended and adopted the Freedom Charter, a declaration of human rights. The great event of the year was the passing of the Senate Act, which reconstituted the Senate, increasing it from 48 to 89, and giving the Government 77 of the 89 seats. So Strijdom secured his two-thirds majority, and passed the Separate Representations of Coloured Voters Act, which the enlarged Appellate Court, increased from five to eleven by the Appellate Court Act, validated on appeal by ten to one, Mr. Justice Schreiner dissenting. Meanwhile white women of South Africa had formed the 'Black Sash', an organization for the defence of the Constitution, and women wearing black sashes as a sign of mourning for the dying Constitution held vigils and 'haunted' Ministers when they opened bridges, conferences and buildings.

Disgusting methods were used by Government officials as they classified people for the Population Register under the Population Registration Act. Combs and pencils were passed through the hair of persons to determine whether they were African or Coloured, and intimate and insulting questions were asked. Parliament passed the Departure from the Union Regulation Act, to regulate the visits abroad of persons likely to harm the Union and its lawful government. Dr. Charles Warren, the Negro member of an American study group, was refused entry to the Union. The long-awaited Tomlinson report, which the Government hoped would justify *apartheid*, was published; but it estimated that in A.D. 2000, white people would still be far outnumbered in the white areas, no matter what the development of the native reserves. The Tomlinson Commission also recommended the spending of over £100,000,000 on the development of the reserves in ten years, whereupon the Government voted £3,500,000. This was a great blow to the total separationists, but they still persist in advocating total separation. The Catholics decided to run their schools unaided, and raised a sum of £750,000, but it remained uncertain whether they would secure the necessary permission. Adams College, the century-old mission school in Natal, though it had secured the necessary finance, was refused permission, and had to close down.

One of the most totalitarian laws of the year was the Natives (Prohibition of Interdicts) Act, which prohibited any court from granting an interdict to any African ordered to remove from an urban location by an order which came or 'purported' to come from the appropriate official; the African resident must first remove himself, and only thereafter could he take proceedings, during which time his job and his home might well have been given to some other person. Not even if the order were served wrongly upon him, not even if the order had been in fact intended for quite some other person, could he obtain an interdict. Still another bad year.

In 1957 the Fort Hare University Transfer Bill and the Separate University Education Bill gave notice of the Government's intention to provide wholly separate university education for non-white students, and to carry out Dr. Malan's threat against the 'open' universities of Capetown and the Witwatersrand, which admitted non-white students. These matters were referred to a Parliamentary Commission, but it is expected that later this year (1958) the Government will provide for the eventual if not immediate total separation of white university education from non-white. The commotion of the year was provided by the famous church clause of the Native Laws Amendment Act, which gave the Minister, after securing the concurrence of the local authority, the right to forbid Africans to attend church services in white urban areas, as well as other rights over attendance of Africans at other places. The church clause was vigorously opposed by the white English-speaking churches, but the Dutch Reformed Churches received assurances from the Minister that satisfied them. Many church leaders advised their followers to disobey the law, a grave action without precedent in our history.

However, later in the year the new Group Areas Act achieved quietly what Dr. Verwoerd had achieved in a glare of world publicity. It defined 'occupation' of an area other than one's own in such a way as to threaten almost any kind of inter-racial association. The Nursing Act created separate racial registers, the whole profession to be controlled by an all-white Council, which was empowered to prescribe different courses for different races, as well as different uniforms and badges. Another bad year.

Just before the General Election of 1958 the first elections for the now separated coloured voters were held. It was estimated that only 30% of the possible total of Coloured voters had bothered to register, and of these only two-fifths voted. It was estimated that young Coloured people boycotted the elections almost completely. The four United

Party candidates won the four seats easily, completely routing the Nationalists, the Liberal Party having decided not to contest the elections. The authoritative view was that only older and more conservative Coloured people had voted, and only a fraction of them, and that they had registered an overwhelming vote against *apartheid*, which was threatening to root them up from their homes and to remind them at every turn of their inferiority to those who had played such a great part in their genesis. It is generally believed that the Coloured people of South Africa have never been so cold in their attitude to the whites.

Then came the General Election. It was won by the Nationalist Party with 103 seats (a gain of 7) against 53 for the United Party (a gain of 1), these Nationalist gains having been made at the expense of the United Party, while the United Party gains were made at the expense of Labour and Independents. Thus the white electorate moved to the right. It is estimated that the votes were divided roughly 50:50 between the Nationalists and the United Party. The Labour Party was wiped out, and the three Liberals, contesting their first parliamentary election, secured respectively 6%, 7% and 17% of the poll.

The African National Congress decided to call a stay-at-home strike for April 14, 15 and 16, the last day being the day of the General Election. The plan had the support of the other Congresses, was advised against by the Liberal Party and was condemned by the Nationalists and the United Party. The Minister of Labour, Mr. Jan de Klerk, threatened to give the strikers a taste of 'white supremacy', and all police were alerted. The strike was a failure and was cancelled on the evening of the first day. It revealed one thing, and that was the vast amount of organization still required by the

African people if they were to exert significant extra-parliamentary pressures. It probably also revealed the great damage that the Government had inflicted on the African National Congress by its namings, bannings and arrests not to mention its legislation.

When the stay-at-home strike was threatening, Dr. Verwoerd, Minister of Native Affairs, invoked the Native Administration Act of 1927, and forbade meetings of more than ten Africans in many areas, in order to prevent labour unrest. This ban is still in operation today (June 22, ten weeks after the election),* and as a consequence the Liberal Party has been unable to hold freely attended meetings. Appeals by the Party to the Secretary for Native Affairs elicited the information that the Minister had been extremely busy, and that he was still gathering information, yet he knew and must have known that the Liberal Party has no record of association with labour unrest. It suits him to keep the Liberal Party waiting on him, that is all; it shows to the Liberal Party, and to any other person who cares to take note, who is the *baas*.

The last striking event in 1958 was the proclamation of group areas in the City of Durban, by which 3,000 Europeans and 97,000 people of other races are to be removed. It is the Indian community which is likely to suffer the most grievous losses; their property, so valuable to them, is of no value to the Europeans to whom the area now belongs. It is true that under the Group Areas Development Act the authorities may assign a 'basic' value to any property, but from their decision there is no appeal. So *apartheid* goes on its cruel and callous way, hiding behind fine words, but leaving a train of bitterness and suffering in its wake.

And now we look forward to the first session of our new

*The ban was lifted on August 29.

Parliament, wondering what new fortifications will be erected, wondering what new folly will be committed in this fantastic process of making Afrikanerdom safe by the most dangerous methods in the world.

CHAPTER VII

NO EASY FUTURE

I HOPE that this brief historical account has helped readers in other countries to understand why Afrikaner Nationalism has become what it is today, and how inflexible it appears to be in the matter of race relations. For some people African Nationalism is the irresistible force, and Afrikaner Nationalism is the immovable obstacle.

Further, this account should have made it clear that the liberal idea of a *common society* is repugnant and repellent to many Afrikaners, and the fact that the idea was introduced by the British administrator and missionary has made it even more so.

And now the Afrikaner Nationalist rules the country and there seems little possibility at the moment of unseating him. As a result of this his doctrines of *apartheid* have been powerfully reinforced, and there can be no doubt that just as in the past Afrikaners were subject to a process of anglicization, so now English-speaking people are subject to a process of Afrikanerization, more particularly in respect of these doctrines.

It is clear from the results of the 1958 elections that half of the white voters are in favour of white baasskap and Afrikaner supremacy, and that those 50% of the voters can win two-thirds of the seats; it would appear that of the other half of the voters, the great majority, though not in favour of Afrikaner supremacy, are certainly in favour of white baasskap, although they do not like the phrase and prefer *white leadership*. It would appear that the white electorate is not in favour of any political concessions to non-white people and that the United Party has, since the deaths of Hofmeyr and Smuts, steadily drifted to the right, through fear of authority or through hopelessness, or even through a growing acceptance of the view that white and black interests are irreconcilable, and that all white people should stand together.

Furthermore it would appear that in Southern Rhodesia the white electorate is moving in the same direction; and might conceivably, after having fled bodily to Rhodesia for freedom, flee back spiritually to South Africa for protection.

These are ugly facts, and they must be faced. They are made still uglier by the possibility, seen so clearly by Hofmeyr, that white action would evoke black counteraction, and that every repressive act would make conflict more and more inevitable.* Hofmeyr said, 'Go forward in faith', but today this would be regarded by the majority of white South Africans as highly unpractical, unrealistic and dangerous.

How does one escape from this predicament, if one really believes that to do justice and to do injustice are equally dangerous? There is one classical escape, and that is through total *apartheid*, the thoroughgoing division of South Africa into separate racial territories, in each of which the racial group in occupation will run its own affairs and pursue its own happiness. The arguments put forward to support total *apartheid* are, *first* that different racial groups cannot live in

*Professor McCrone, of the University of the Witwatersrand, is the outstanding exponent of this theme.

harmony in a common territory, *second* that subordinate groups will never receive justice in a common territory. Nor do I doubt that fear of ultimate disaster is an important motive.

Professor B. B. Keet has called this the pipe-dream, and no name could be more appropriate, not merely because the dream is fanciful, but also because it can be dreamed even when every sign points, every event moves, in a contrary direction. There are I think four insuperable reasons why total *apartheid* is impossible; there is no land for it, there is no money for it, there is no time for it, there is no will for it.

Nevertheless the smokers of this pipe would argue that it is the liberal vision of a common society open to all that is in fact the true pipe-dream. There is nothing, they would argue, in the 300 years of our history to indicate that such an end is possible.

What is more, some of the frustrated opponents of the Government, after the still greater defeat of the 1958 elections, are inclined to say, '*Apartheid* is too strong for us; it's a waste of time to fight it, let's try to work it.'

Finally, the total apartheider can say, 'I am a liberal too. I'm the Afrikaner liberal. I want *apartheid*, but I want a just *apartheid*. Why don't you support me? I at least am in contact with the sources of power.'

There are clear and emphatic reasons why liberals of my persuasion are totally unable to lend support to the forces of total *apartheid*, quite apart from the fact that there is no land, money, time or will for it.

To us *apartheid*, of whatever brand, is a rejection of one's fellow men, not those of Kamchatka and Patagonia, but those who are born and live and die in the same land. To make *apartheid* total does not fundamentally alter the fact that it is a rejection. Total *apartheid* is a device whereby one can have in imagination rejection and justice simultaneously. Seen from a religious point of view, total *apartheid* is love of one's neighbour, provided he does not live next door.

Our present society has been the joint product of all South Africa; but some of these assets are quite indivisible; for example, our cities and harbours, our mines. How could there be any just division of the country? On the contrary we believe that these new societies will be condemned forever to a poor and inferior life. Therefore we reject the proposition. Further, having seen the suffering and injustice inflicted by the preliminary measures of *apartheid*, how can we possibly believe that the final measures will be something quite different? *Apartheid*, whether partial or total, is essentially something done by someone with power to someone with none.

But we reject it even more emphatically because we believe that the vain pursuit of it will postpone still further the day when all South Africans share equally the duties, privileges and joys of living in South Africa. And to that we may add that the pursuit of this goal of fantasy will turn aside some of our best minds from consideration of the real problem of creating a common society under outstandingly difficult circumstances.

We have another reason for believing that total *apartheid* is a fantasy; for, supposing it could be achieved, how could the white State watch with equanimity the forging of alliances between the non-white State and other countries of Africa and the world?

This demonstrates the difficulty of our problem. The *apartheider* says that the idea of a *common society* is unthinkable, impossible, perhaps even disgusting. The liberal says that *apartheid* as domination is doomed to die, and *apartheid* as total separation is doomed never to be born. It is my experience that the total *apartheider*, in whom reason and emotion struggle incessantly, sees the truth of the liberal argument, and is driven to a further and new argument, namely that so long as we do not know with certainty whether total *apartheid* or integration will be the solution, it is our duty to drive towards total *apartheid* rather than integration, because from the first there can be a turning-back, but never from the second. This is an interesting and significant argument.

It is my duty to place clearly before the reader the difficulties in the way of attaining either of these goals. It is also my duty to explain that there are many South Africans who, believing it impossible to reach either goal, are deeply pessimistic about the future. And it will be my duty a little later to contend that while total *apartheid* is impossible, a democratic society is inevitable, unless democracy dies out in the world. Just how we reach that society, and whether it will be reached without a bitter price, such as the ejection of most white persons or the suffering of an Algerian agony—those are the real questions. Whether one stays to work for that society regardless of the consequences, or whether one leaves the country fearful of the consequences, is to my mind as much a question of character and temperament as it is of being able to predict the future and to act upon that prediction.

There is another difficulty in the way of achieving a democratic and non-racial and liberal solution. One of the reasons why one supports the liberal solution is because one sees the danger of group irreconcilability. But the very growth of this group irreconcilability makes the liberal solution less likely and more difficult to bring about. My readers should by this time see quite clearly that the Government disapproves of inter-racial or non-racial association; it has already taken certain *indirect* steps to make it impossible, and it has power in certain circumstances to take *direct* steps also. It does not wish however to say boldly, so that the world can hear, 'There must be no friendship or human communication between a white and a non-white person';* but it feels able to say, 'You, a white person, may not enter that area, because that area is set aside for black persons, so that they may live self-respecting, self-reliant, self-supporting lives, without let or hindrance from any person of any other group or race.' In fact, long before this Government came to power, no white person could enter a 'location' without permission; and a location superintendent would be incredulous if a white person sought a permit to pay a friendly call on a black person in a location. In other words, the increasing amount of enforced racial separation makes it more and more difficult to create that racial understanding on which any solution must be based.

Fortunately the road ahead is not completely blocked. S.A.B.R.A.,† at its most recent conference at Stellenbosch, was most outspoken on the subject of consultation between white and non-white people, and decided to call a conference with non-white leaders in the near future. This is in direct conflict with the policy of Dr. Verwoerd, who told students at Stellenbosch that they should leave consultation to himself and his Department, and should not be carried away by so-called broadminded ideas. It was in fact strongly rumoured at the S.A.B.R.A. Conference that Dr. Verwoerd had resigned from the Bureau, but this fact has never been confirmed or denied.

*I have no doubt that Dr. Verwoerd, if he had sole power, would have no hesitation in framing a law which would say categorically 'no non-white person shall enter a white person's house except in the capacity of a servant.'

†I remind the reader that S.A.B.R.A., the South African Bureau of Racial Affairs, is a non-political organization supported largely by Nationalists of the total *apartheid* belief.

What is more, there are hopes that S.A.B.R.A. will really consult 'leaders', and not the stooges that Dr. Verwoerd consults. By leaders I mean people like ex-Chief Luthuli and Professor Z. K. Matthews, both of whom were arrested on charges of high treason in December, 1956. Professor L. J. Duplessis, another S.A.B.R.A. man, bluntly called Dr. Verwoerd's consultants 'hirelings', and that is precisely what they are.

Nevertheless, however cheering this may be, consultation between S.A.B.R.A. and non-white leaders is likely to be more palatable to the Government than consultation between liberals and non-white leaders, because S.A.B.R.A. is committed to a policy of total *apartheid*. One therefore cannot exclude the possibility that the law will be applied in such a way that only that kind of inter-racial association will be permitted which meets to promote racial separation.

A last question must be faced before we proceed to discuss the task of Liberalism and of the Liberal Party in the present situation. All of us hope that whatever difficult times must be endured, South Africa will eventually become a democracy; and by that we mean a country with parliamentary institutions based on universal suffrage, with a written constitution and a bill of rights, and a distribution of power and authority, not only in respect of parliament, cabinet and judiciary, but also in respect of national, provincial and local bodies.

This goal will almost certainly be reached if democracy does not retreat throughout the world. But it may be reached in one of two ways, either as an aftermath of violence and revolution resulting in a black racial domination, or by an evolutionary process of a massive kind. To put it bluntly, the choice is not simply revolution or evolution, it is revolution or revolutionary evolution. If some readers do not like that language, one can say the choice is between revolution and massive evolution. I do not know one liberal who believes that change will come about as a result of steady and quiet evolution. That particular fantasy is cherished only by those who think the change will or should take a thousand years (or some comparable time); it is often called the ostrich-fantasy, and it is held, I believe, by those whose vested interest depends on stability, and/or those who hope never to see such change. It is a common United Party view.

If we are fated to pass through a violent revolutionary period, it is clear I think that no liberal organization will survive it, and perhaps no liberal either. That there will be a task for liberalism in the period of aftermath, I have no doubt whatsoever, that is, if democracy still lives stoutly in the world. But that is a matter for the future. I shall concern myself rather with the task of liberals and a Liberal Party in a period of massive evolution. I believe in fact that we have already entered such a period, and it is clearly the duty of liberals, not only to themselves, but to every person in South Africa, to endeavour to ensure, in collaboration with all like-minded people, that the process is not allowed to enter a violent and chaotic phase, during which all liberty would be lost, with no guarantee as to when it would be found again.

This is no easy task; it is not unlike being required to guide safely to its destination a vehicle over whose steering one has control, but over whose speed one has not.

CHAPTER VIII

PARLIAMENTARY AND
EXTRA-PARLIAMENTARY FUNCTIONS

THE Liberal Party in South Africa therefore rejected the policy of white supremacy, primarily because it was immoral, but also because it was impossible. It rejected the policy of total *apartheid*, primarily because it was impossible, but also because it was immoral. It rejected the United Party policy of 'discrimination with justice', on the grounds, justifiable I believe, that one could get better discrimination from the Nationalists, and better justice from the Liberals themselves.* The Party also rejected the revolutionary solution, partly through temperament, partly through belief that revolution would destroy the fundamental freedoms of man.

The Party sees itself as participating in and assisting the process of evolution, and insists on the possibility of evolutionary change, though it does not believe this can be a process of planned gradualism. Indeed there is one overwhelmingly sound reason for believing that planned gradualism is impossible, and that is that the Nationalist Party will, by all ordinary reckoning, never again be defeated at an election. This opinion is held strongly both

---

*I realize that the word 'discrimination' may not necessarily mean 'discrimination against'. But the word as used by the United Party means 'discrimination against', because the Party supports legislation by which one section of the population imposes segregation upon the others.

inside and outside the Nationalist Party. The reader already knows of the rural underloading and the urban overloading, by which a rural constituency need contain only 85% of the number of voters obtained by dividing the total number of voters in the Union by the total number of constituencies; conversely, an urban constituency may be overloaded up to 115% of this average quota. This favours the Nationalist Party because the rural districts are overwhelmingly Afrikaans-speaking and overwhelmingly Nationalist. The reader should also remember that the white population is nearly two-thirds Afrikaans-speaking, that the Afrikaner birthrate is higher than the English-speaking birthrate, and that the younger generations of Afrikaners become more and more Nationalist because of their separate Afrikaans-medium schools and their separate Afrikaans-medium universities, many of which, it may be said, have taught consistently that an Afrikaner cannot be a good one unless he is a Nationalist. Further, in 1936 General Hertzog removed African voters to a separate roll, and in 1956 Mr. Strijdom removed Coloured voters also, thus concentrating potential support for the Opposition in a limited number of constituencies; and it is not unlikely that the first roll will soon be abolished, and the second will not be long in following it. Then South-West Africa was granted a wholly disproportionate representation, and returned a grand slam of Nationalists to Parliament. The Senate was fantastically enlarged, and a new method of election introduced, whereby the Government took 77 of the 89 seats, thus giving Mr. Strijdom a manufactured two-thirds majority in both Houses sitting together.

How under these circumstances will the Nationalists ever be ejected by parliamentary means? The fact is, they have deliberately set out to make it virtually impossible. Legally and constitutionally, they have made South Africa a one-party state.

The massive nature of Nationalist entrenchments is such that it has compelled all the elements of the Opposition to reconsider their strategy. How does one oppose a Government which has given to its own supporters every conceivable advantage, and which seems unlikely to be unseated unless some event or series of events should occur which would compel white South Africa to reconsider its course?

The Liberal Party, when confronted by this problem, has always maintained that even under these difficult circumstances it has a parliamentary as well as an extra-parliamentary duty. The parliamentary duty is to try to put its policies and principles before the white voters of the country; to try to persuade white voters that failure to change their attitudes can lead only to disaster; to uphold the claims of justice and to preach both the folly and the wrongness of race-discrimination; to bring African and Indian and Coloured and European Liberals onto the election platforms, thus giving largely white audiences an opportunity to see that those values of which they wrongly suppose themselves to be the sole custodians (and of which they sometimes wrongly suppose themselves to be custodians at all)—to see that those values, I repeat, are supported by their fellow South Africans of other races, and to be reassured that a non-racial democracy is a valid and exciting choice.

The Liberal Party has always attached great importance to the fact that its membership is open to all. I read not long since an African's cynical description of 'inter-racial association' as 'occasionally inviting some cleaner natives to tea'. For many members of the Party, inter-racial association has meant entering into a new country, exciting, dangerous and beautiful. It seems likely to become more dangerous, because there is no doubt that the Minister of Native Affairs and numberless thousands of his supporters regard inter-racial association as something unnatural and disgusting, to be forbidden by law. Political association is the worst of all, because obviously those who indulge in it are hostile to *apartheid*, and white 'agitators' corrupt 'decent natives' and give them ideas which undermine the ideal and separated society for which the Minister is working. As I have stated earlier, in this year, 1958, on April 11, the Minister forbade the gathering of more than ten Africans together except for certain harmless purposes, and he gave as his reason for so doing the need 'to prevent irresponsible elements during the coming days or weeks from causing labour unrest by the holding of meetings. It was the wish of the Minister that as far as his Department was concerned, the notice should remain in effect only temporarily, in other words, for just as long as was necessary in the areas concerned.' As I write (June 22, 1958) the ban is still in force, and organizers of Liberal Party or other meetings have either had to limit the number of Africans attending, or to cancel the meetings. When questioned as to whether there was still a danger of labour unrest, the Secretary for Native Affairs replied to the Party that the Minister had been too busy to re-examine the position. It is to be expected therefore that sooner or later mixed meetings may be forbidden altogether, and this is likely to be done *indirectly*, so that critics overseas can be informed by the State Information Office that this is only an isolated case of inconvenience, which could be righted only at the expense of setting aside a law which ensures the happiness of millions of non-white people, who at last have been given separate areas of peace and opportunity where they may lead unfettered lives of bliss, free from all the humiliations and deprivations that they suffered when they were forced to live in a mixed society.

We do not expect therefore that the future of inter-racial association, particularly when it is for political purposes, is likely to be easy. For one thing, the purely physical barriers of *apartheid* make it difficult; but in addition to that, inter-racial association is assuming—some would say has already assumed—the form of treason. No less a person than the Prime Minister has called opposition to *apartheid* by this name, thus making people more and more afraid of being associated with any deviation.*

Such a choice of what one believes to be just and good and what others believe to be treason, calls for grave decisions. But there are liberals, and I hope to be found amongst them, who, faced by the choice between conformity on the one hand and the assertion of one's right to associate with whom one will, no matter what the penalties, would choose to assert their right. For the Christian liberal the choice should be simple, being between obedience to God and obedience to man, but it will not thereby be made easier. And we must face the position soberly that many white Christians in South Africa find it easier as time goes on, and as the Government becomes more powerful, to believe that *apartheid* and the great commandments can be happily reconciled, and that Christ would have approved *apartheid* had he been here. They therefore cease to fight or to protest against injustice, because they dare not admit that it exists. Furthermore it becomes easier for them to dismiss supporters of human rights as subversive and communistic,

*I recall a tragic case in the Cape Peninsula, where a man, happily married and with children, living as a white man, was suddenly declared under the Population Registration Act to be coloured. The tragic aspect was that the wife, who had been happily married to him for 20 years, in this time of crisis decided to stick to her race and not to her husband. An even more tragic, and bitterly ironic, aspect was that the children also fled from the father, outraged by what he had done to them. Yet they cannot really flee from him, because they are now coloured too.

or if they do not wish to go that far, as unrealistic and impractical.

►◄

Let us return to the topic of the Liberal and parliamentary action, that is, to the whole question of trying to get representatives into Parliament, where they will oppose vigorously the policies of the present Government. This we have accepted as part of our duty, but it certainly raises an important problem. By getting into Parliament one hopes at least to influence policy, one hopes to influence the progress of South Africa from a white-dominated state to a non-racial democracy. One must therefore answer the question, 'You hope to persuade white South Africa to move from a situation in which all political power is in white hands, to a situation where all responsible people exercise political power. What do you propose as the first move?'*

This in fact is the matter of the franchise, the most difficult question confronting any political party that finds no solution in *apartheid*, whether total or of the 'baasskap' variety.

The Liberal Party, having decided that it had a parliamentary duty, had to express itself on the matter of the franchise, and it had to do so at an early stage of its existence, when its members were little known to one another, and when they were bound together more by their opposition

---

*The United Party has always evaded this issue by declaring that non-white people are not interested in franchises but in food and shelter. This is partially true, but there are two objections to it, the first being that there is an obvious connection in South Africa between political power and standard of living, the second being that non-white leaders are profoundly interested in the franchise even if some are afraid (civil servants, for example) to be so openly. Both United Party and Nationalist Party reply to this second objection that the more courageous non-white leaders are 'agitators', secondly that they are not representative. All leaders of the African National Congress are regarded by the Government as being not representative.

to injustice than by their common championship of any political solution. Eventually, in 1953 (very soon after its founding) the Party decided to put forward a qualified franchise, independent of race and colour, but dependent on education, property, earning power and, failing any of these, a record of a decent and industrious life; the educational qualification was made Standard VI.

This decision was not acceptable to all. There were some—not many—who wanted a higher educational qualification; there were some who wanted no qualification at all. These latter argued that we were not facing any normal situation, but a veritable parting of the ways; the choice was not of what kind of man was acceptable as a voter, but of what kind of man was acceptable as a man. It was not a qualified vote that the African was asking for, but to be recognized as a man, once and for all.

Therefore the Party in 1954 declared that universal suffrage was its goal, but it continued to recognize that it might be necessary to achieve this by stages during a transitional period, during which there would be qualifications 'that should apply for the minimum period necessary for a smooth transition to universal adult suffrage'.

This policy still frightens many white voters, just as it fails to satisfy more radical persons (both inside and outside the Party) because of its qualifying clauses.

Yet in a way this is the inevitable dilemma* of a bridge-building party in an *apartheid* country.

---

*There is no organization without its dilemma, except the totalitarian one which allows no choices. The very bringing together of different persons to pursue similar aims is productive of dilemmas. One of the dilemmas of the Nationalists is immigration, which could strengthen the white population, but would probably also strengthen the United Party. One of the dilemmas of the United Party is shown in its slogan 'discrimination with justice'. One of the dilemmas of the African National Congress is whether to oppose Nationalism for the evil it has done to the African people or whether to espouse a vigorous nationalism of its own.

There are only two other courses open. The first is to retreat to a cautious policy of offering franchise concessions to qualified non-white people, in which case one must forfeit the trust of their political leaders, and therefore render one's work of bridge-building altogether futile.

The other course is to leave white South Africa to its own devices, and to identify oneself solely with non-white aspirations. Such a course, unmodified by other considerations, does not appeal to Liberals; it not only does not appeal to white Liberals, it fails to appeal to non-white Liberals also. At all costs we intend to proceed on the assumption that there is a valuable group in the white population that must not be jettisoned, and we look forward to a new South Africa where all groups of the population will be represented without discrimination or privilege in the activities and councils of the nation.

▶◀

There are good grounds for supposing that non-white South Africans will never again accept a qualified franchise, and that they will accept only a universal franchise (perhaps with or perhaps without any stages), and a written constitution embodying a bill of rights and subject to amendment only under the most exacting circumstances. These reasons I give now, and they are also excellent reasons why a white Liberal should feel it repugnant to put forward a qualified franchise. The reasons are that this country has had a qualified franchise for over a hundred years, and that in respect of Africans and Coloured people the restrictions and qualifications have been progressively increased to the point where no one would be surprised to see the franchise abolished altogether; while concurrently the franchise for Europeans has become less and less qualified; until we expect (on high authority) to hear of the enfranchisement of 18-year-olds at any moment.*

The Cape Colony was given representative government in 1853, but by 1887 Rhodes had made it impossible for Africans who held land in communal tenure (i.e. tribal Africans, often called contemptuously 'blanket kaffirs') to exercise the vote. In 1892 he raised the property qualification, and imposed an education test, both of which steps had the approval of the first J. H. Hofmeyr. In 1909 W. P. Schreiner went to England to protest against the unsatisfactory way in which the non-white franchise was to be entrenched in the new Act of Union, for he declared the two-thirds majority required for any change to be no safeguard at all. His fears were justified, for in 1936, as I have already pointed out, General Hertzog secured the two-thirds majority and removed all African voters to a separate roll, with the right to elect three white M.P.s and four white Senators. In 1955 Mr. Strijdom manufactured a two-thirds majority by enlarging the Senate on undemocratic and unprecedented lines and removed the Coloured voters to a separate roll. And already from high quarters has come the warning that perhaps the Government will soon abolish African representation in Parliament altogether.

How can one again in 1958 propose a franchise of a kind which was introduced in 1853, and withered altogether away? It is impossible.

The fear that motivates this whittling away of rights is of course understandable. It is the fear that generosity or statesmanship of any kind leads sooner or later to 'swamping'. It is said of course that the fear is really otherwise; and is rather the fear of imperilling the civilized

*This has now been done.

standards of one's society; but it goes deeper than that—it is the fear of being 'swamped' by a black majority, who, however civilized, will seek revenge for past wrongs.

Will a black majority seek revenge for past wrongs? Alternatively, will it adopt repressive policies towards white citizens? One can reply to this question with one reassurance, that at least a black majority will not have the motive that has been behind all the repressive legislation of the Nationalists, namely, the fear of being 'swamped'.

►◄

A true liberal does not in fact think in terms of groups, he thinks in terms of persons. Is this unpractical, idealistic, sentimental, unrealistic? The Liberal thinks it is the only way to think if one is working for a non-racial democracy.

Is this the way to get votes? At Sea Point, Mr. Gerald Gordon presented the case for the goal of a universal franchise, and gained the support of 17% of those who voted. In other words, 17% of those white people who voted in Sea Point were willing to consider living in a society where neither privilege nor power will depend on the colour of one's skin.

Will Mr. Gerald Gordon, or any other Liberal, ever win Sea Point? That we do not know. But we think it is important, no matter what the future may be, to rally those white South African forces that are willing to play their part in a new democratic society, whose duties and privileges are open to all.

►◄

One last question. Is it really practical or sensible to put before a white electorate such an extreme goal as that of the universal franchise, even with qualifications? Should one not be putting before them a safer and more gradual programme, so that one would have a better chance of winning a seat, and influencing the councils of Parliament?

In some other society, no doubt, it is the right thing to lead the electorate away from a dangerous course by gentle and gradual means. South Africa is not a normal society, and there is no time for gentle and gradual means. The choice, as I indicated before, is not between revolution and gradualism, but between revolution and a massive evolution.

Will we win? We do not know, but even if we do not, we consider that the organizing of liberal opinion now, both white and non-white, must affect the end result. Therefore we will continue as long as we are able to perform a parliamentary duty. Meanwhile let us proceed to consider those duties which are called extra-parliamentary, a word, I may add, which has for many white South Africans an unjustifiably terrifying sound.

I shall close this chapter with a brief observation. The Nationalist Government of South Africa has made it virtually impossible for any opposition to unseat it by parliamentary means. But while it has done this, it pretends it has not, and takes a stern view of any of its opponents who suggest that under the circumstances one is compelled to examine extra-parliamentary means. In other words, having made the parliamentary game unwinnable for its opponents, it insists that they should go on playing it.

That is why so many white opponents of the Government who think of politics as purely a white man's game have given up all hope; and having given up all hope, they are in danger of supporting, through sheer hopelessness, the very Government which took their hope away.

No white South African can ever hope to oppose the Nationalist Government successfully if he looks upon politics as only a white man's game, because no one will ever be able to play that game better than the Nationalists can play it.

CHAPTER IX

THE ROLE OF THE LIBERAL PARTY

IT stands to reason that much political activity in South Africa cannot be parliamentary at all. Seeing that nearly 80% of the people have no ordinary franchise, and seeing that the Government threatens to abolish, in whole or in part, what franchise they have, it is not surprising that most of their political activity should be extra-parliamentary. It is parties such as the United Party, and pre-eminently the Nationalist Party, who want politics to be parliamentary, and who tend to regard as subversive any person or organization that talks of an extra-parliamentary duty. What is more, they are able to pull the wool over the eyes of white people elsewhere, who wonder at the absence of non-white persons in Parliament, by persuading them that the colour bar is not an offensive institution, but a veritable bulwark of civilization and democracy.

Now Afrikaner Nationalism is not in the all-powerful position that it appears to be from the parliamentary viewpoint. It commands the support of only half of the 3,000,000 white people of the country, and beyond that secures the unwilling compliance of 11,000,000 non-white people, some of whom have no great political knowledge, but know very well what it means to be pushed around, sometimes politely, sometimes with the extreme of cruelty. Of the 2,500,000,000 people of the outside world, only in places such as Kenya, Mississippi, Algeria, would any support for *apartheid* be found.

Afrikaner Nationalism is well aware of the insecurity of its tenure. Even now, at the very height of its power, Minister Jan de Klerk, speaking at Brits on June 21, 1958, said, 'We must fight until the bitter end and support Mr. Strijdom, just as an Aaron and Hur of old held the arms of Moses aloft.' Mr. de Klerk, proud to be known as 'Blood River' de Klerk, is continually reminding Afrikaners that they dare not relax.

This theme is only too well known. Afrikaner Nationalism must have its enemies even while it fears them. It must never feel safe, because then it will cease to be vigilant.

This has led some of its opponents to argue that Afrikaner Nationalism must never be too strongly opposed, for then it will turn and rend its enemies still more fiercely. This argument can be heard in many opposition circles, and even in overseas countries; and it has a variation to the effect that the more security Afrikaner Nationalism achieves, the more urbane and tolerant it will become.

This I think is false. Afrikaner Nationalism will never be secure. Its great strength springs solely from its insecurity. But its insecurity is not thereby lessened, because its great strength can never be great enough. I am one of those who believes that Afrikaner Nationalism, not for want of courage but for lack of this ultimate strength, would not stand up to any real and sustained challenge to its baasskap. It would, as the British had to do in India, have to adapt itself to new circumstances. Afrikaner Nationalism must therefore be resolutely opposed.

Liberals would however never wish to destroy the Afrikaner people, nor to interfere with their language, nor to prevent the observance of custom and tradition which did not involve the pushing of other people around. Afrikaner Nationalism has a hard lesson to learn; it must survive, as it did in the past, because of its inner strength, not because of its protective laws. In the new society we envisage every Afrikaner will be given the same protection of fundamental human rights as is enjoyed by any other citizen.

Liberalism is not opposed, as some people suppose, to the 'own-sort-ness' of nationalism, but it is utterly opposed to the enforcement of 'own-sort-ness' by the State, which goes even to the extent of deciding what the 'own-sort-ness' of any person should be, and which prevents a parent from having his child educated in the language of his choice. Liberalism is opposed to Afrikaner Nationalism, not because it seeks to ensure Afrikaner survival, but because it seeks to do so at the expense of other groups. Liberalism would be utterly false to its ideals if it did not oppose Afrikaner Nationalism as embodied in the Nationalist Government.

There is today in South Africa a great reluctance on the part of opposition groups to say or do anything which will hurt Afrikaner susceptibilities. This is partly because decent people are always careful of racial generalizations, partly because the Afrikaner Nationalist Government is so powerful. But it is the Afrikaner Nationalist who insists that he and his Government are one, and there is no point in evading the issue. Afrikaner Nationalists and their Government are responsible for *apartheid* legislation, some of which is evil and cruel. Therefore they must be opposed by all lovers of freedom, and, seeing that they have entrenched themselves parliamentarily, they must be opposed in other ways.

►◄

The role of the Liberal Party (and of other liberals where the role is not party political) is to strengthen at every point the opposition to Nationalism. This does not mean the formation of a unitary common front, but it does mean a common front in so far as opposition to race discrimination is concerned. What real opposition can there be to Afrikaner Nationalism unless it be the opposition of defenders of democracy of whatever race or colour? It is here that the United Party can never offer a real opposition to National-ism, in that it cannot conceive of a co-defence of democratic values and of liberty made by white and non-white together. That was the weakness of the Torch Commando, which, though fighting for the rights of coloured men, would not allow coloured men to join the Commando. These para-doxes are understandable; they are the mark of white South Africa, which shrinks from the idea of making common cause with any non-white person against a fellow white South African. It is a mixture of 'don't quarrel in front of the children' and 'don't quarrel in the face of the enemy'.*

▶◀

In spite of these adverse factors, the cause of multi-racial or non-racial democracy has been advanced, and has assumed a firmer character in recent years. Such co-operation has always existed, but some people today are inclined to sneer at the liberalism of earlier times, just as some American Negroes are inclined to sneer at Booker Washington. One of the pioneers in the modern field was the white Congress of Democrats, which was founded in 1952 and which

*It is one of the great fears of many white defenders of non-white rights that they might be compelled, in case of civil conflagration, to defend themselves against those whom they have always championed.

established firm links with the African National Congress, the South African Indian Congress and the Coloured Peoples Organization; these formed the 'Congress Movement', and it was this movement that was responsible for the holding of the Congress of the People in 1955. This Congress produced the Freedom Charter, a document of human rights of a truly democratic character, with the debatable exception of a few passages advocating the nationalization of land, banks and certain industries, which seemed to necessitate a measure of central control not acceptable to liberals. The holding of the Congress of the People was a courageous action, and was in part responsible for the arrest of many of the leading participants on grounds of high treason; 156 persons were arrested, over sixty were released after the preparatory examination, and over ninety face the trial itself, which began in August, 1958.

The Liberal Party itself, though invited at a later stage in the arrangements, declined to attend the Congress of the People; but it was angered by the arrests, and its National Chairman—at that time myself—joined such non-party personalities as the Bishop of Johannesburg, Judge Lucas and Dr. Ellen Hellman in sponsoring a Defence Fund for the assistance of those arrested.

I think it is necessary for a clear understanding of the relationship between the Liberal Party and the Congress of Democrats to say something about these two bodies, co-operation between whom is an important factor in the fight against *apartheid*. It is necessary to understand that they pursue separate and independent courses, and that the Liberal Party was founded when the Congress of Democrats was already in existence, which seems to show that each represents different temperaments and social theories. It is not my intention however to take any partisan stand;

I wish not so much to compare the two bodies as to make clear their relationship, because many observers overseas find it disconcerting that there should be two separate organizations to represent what appears to them to be essentially the same view.

I think it is a fair observation that the nature of the liberal attitude itself is one of the main causes of difference. The Congress is more disciplined, and the Party less so; the Congress has a more clearly defined opinion and devotes less time to discussion and argument; the Congress prefers the strength of unity to the riches of diversity. This difference is reflected in social theory also, for the Congress attaches importance to an efficient state machinery, while the Party attaches importance to the freedom of individual persons. Some members of the Congress would regard the Party's devotion to freedom as cautious and conservative, while some members of the Party would regard the Congress's espousal of human rights as only a part of a larger strategy. That both organizations are haters of race discrimination there can be no doubt; but one of them would root out race discrimination by a radical reconstruction of society, and the other by the distribution of power and the entrenchment of rights. These differences seem to cause, or to be caused by, or at least to accord with, certain differences of temperament that make close co-operation not always easy to maintain. But it is clear to me that if this co-operation is not maintained, the common cause, genuinely cherished by both, will suffer. I might add one more observation, and that is that the African and Indian Congresses have been able to bring the Congress of Democrats and the Liberal Party into a closer relationship more easily than they could have done it themselves, and I ascribe this to the fact that the African and Indian Congresses contain a wider cross-section of views, and are more used to the reconciling of diverse elements for the sake of a common goal.

Nor must one exclude the fact that the Liberal Party arrived later in the field than the Congress of Democrats, and this in itself caused some difficulty; why did the ally arrive late at the battle, and why did he bring another banner when he came?

However the question was—is co-operation between Liberals and Congressmen possible for the one purpose of fighting race discrimination? Progress towards such co-operation was hastened by the holding of a conference of prominent Africans in Bloemfontein in October 1956, under the auspices of the Interdenominational African Ministers Federation (I.D.A.M.F.) for the purpose of discussing the Tomlinson Report. This notable conference produced some notable documents, from which I make the following quotations.

'This conference does not subscribe to the view that the choice before South Africa consists only of two alternatives—"ultimate complete integration" or "ultimate complete separation between European and Bantu" [quotations from the Tomlinson Report]. The Conference maintains that a proper reading of the South African situation calls for co-operation and interdependence between the various races comprising the South African nation and denies that this arrangement would constitute a threat to the survival of the white man in South Africa.'

And further,

'This conference is convinced that the present policy of *apartheid* constitutes a threat to race relations in the country. Therefore, in the interests of all the people and the future of the country, this conference calls upon all national organizations to mobilize all people, irrespective of race, colour or creed, to form a united front against *apartheid.*'

As a first step towards the establishment of such a 'united front', the Conference suggested the holding of a further conference, embracing all races, as soon as possible.

From that time onward the Liberal Party, as well as Congressmen and non-Congressmen, the Labour Party, non-party liberals and prominent churchmen worked for a multi-racial conference, which was held in Johannesburg in December 1957. The emphasis of the Conference throughout was on the multi-racial character of our country, the injustice and futility of *apartheid*, the importance of the written constitution and the Bill of Rights, and the franchise open to all. The conference was watched throughout by the Security Branch of the Police, although the Committee would not allow them to enter the hall. The proceedings throughout were characterized by dignity and determination, and differences, whether of temperament or politics, were constructively discussed.

▶◀

It is part and parcel of the policy of the Liberal Party to give its full support to the Multi-racial Conference and to all that it stands for. It seems to the Party to be abundantly clear that a non-racial society is the only one that offers hope for the future, with a constitution guaranteeing basic human rights. It, therefore, will work for the maintenance of the Multi-racial Conference, and its support of the Congress movement will be expressed in that way, or in any other way that ensures support for the same ideals.

It will be the policy of the Party to give all possible

support to the African National Congress (A.N.C.), which has pledged its support to a democratic non-racial society. At this point it seems fitting—and here I shall avoid any improper discussion of the intimate affairs of a friendly organization—to consider briefly the dilemmas which are characteristic of such a body as the A.N.C.

The A.N.C. is a non-party organization, and therefore contains in its ranks at least three sections of opinion. One believes that only the radical transformation of society can achieve any useful purpose; another believes in the extension of the rights and duties of democracy to every adult person and entrenchment of those rights; while a third section is tempted to oppose Afrikaner Nationalism by African nationalism, with a policy of 'Africa for the Africans' which might be interpreted as meaning 'Africa for those who lived in Africa before the Europeans and Asians came'. A Liberal could endorse only the second of these policies if a choice had to be made, and it therefore will be the duty of the Party, not to try to disrupt the Congress, but to give its full support to those who stand for the extension of democratic rights. That indeed is what it already does.

The Party would find it difficult to support the United Party, or even the Federal Party, except on particular issues. The fact that both these parties have a colour bar, ideological or merely 'realistic', makes close co-operation difficult. In any event, the United Party would find support from the Liberal Party embarrassing, especially if it persists in its mistaken view that it can win more support in the rural constituencies; for any association with the Liberal Party would be a severe handicap. Closer association with the Federal Party is only less difficult; the Federal Party is largely an anti-republican body, which believes that only deter- mined opposition from the English-speaking people of

Natal can prevent a republic. In conversations with the Liberals, the Federal Party maintains that one should fight the republic *first*, that if necessary one should ensure the secession of Natal *first*; only thereafter, it argues, would it be sensible to talk of the extension of democratic rights to non-white peoples.

The Liberal Party is unable to accept this argument, even although it can be most persuasively put forward. It argues that the Federals, if they ultimately mean to make the seceded state of Natal a non-racial state, must say so now. It argues that the Federals are inspired largely by a uni-racial pro-British, pro-Commonwealth, pro-Crown senti-ment, and that this is no adequate foundation for an African state. Furthermore the Liberal Party stands unequivocally for the rights of Indians to be treated as full citizens, and it is aware that the pro-British backers of the Federal Party in Natal have never championed the rights of Indians. There-fore it sees no reason to believe that a seceded Natal would be any more liberal than, for example, the City Council of the great city of Durban, which lent its full support to the evil Group Areas Act, which seeks, if not the destruction, then at least the segregation and impoverishment of the Indian community.

The Liberal Party attitude to the republic is unequivocal. It 'holds that a republic shall not come into being unless it is the express desire of a majority of all adult persons, regardless of race and colour, voting together in a referen-dum'. It 'is opposed to all authoritarian forms of govern-ment, particularly the republican government as envisaged by the 1942 draft constitution' put forward by the Nation-alist Party. Furthermore the attitude of the Liberal Party towards the Commonwealth is also unequivocal. It main-tains that 'it is in the interests of South Africa as a sovereign ndependent state to maintain and safeguard its ties with the Commonwealth'.

Therefore the attitude of the Liberal Party towards the Federal Party is plain. It supports the Federal Party in its opposition to the republic, not because it opposes the establishment of a republic as such, but because it opposes the establishment of the race-discriminatory republic that the Nationalist Party wants. Its attitude to the United Party is also plain; it hopes to attract to its own ranks the more liberal members of that party. Should the United Party itself be drawn nearer to the Nationalists, and should it lend more and more support to the policies of *apartheid*, and should its liberal members as a consequence resign or be thrown out, then it earnestly hopes that these liberal members would see the folly of establishing yet another party between the United Party and the Liberals, with the inevitable but absurd policy of 'discrimination with still more justice'.

><

The relations of the Liberal Party to the Indian Congress have grown closer and closer, largely as a result of the total opposition of the Party to the Group Areas Act, and the wholehearted acceptance of the Indian community as South Africans in the fullest sense. I do not suggest that the opposition of the Congress of Democrats is any less whole-hearted; on the contrary the plight of the Indian community has proved to be the strongest binding element uniting the Party with the Congress of Democrats.

The defeat of Mr. Alex Hepple and Mr. Leo Lovell, the Labour candidates in the 1958 elections, was a great blow to the Liberal cause. We wish there could be a closer relationship, even a coalescence, between Liberals and Labour. We believe they could educate us in economic affairs, just as we believe—humbly I hope—that we have something to offer by virtue of our total rejection of racial discrimination. Our respect for the Labour Party members of Parliament was unbounded, but it seems that they look for a more 'realistic' realignment. They should look for it on the basis of total rejection of the colour bar, and they should join us, and add to our strength their magnificent gifts.

Our relations with the South African Coloured People's Organization (S.A.C.P.O.) are sketchy, and are largely the responsibility of our Cape Division. So far we have neither won much Coloured support for Liberalism, which is not surprising in view of the wasting away of the coloured franchise, nor have we established firm relations with S.A.C.P.O. This remains one of the great challenges to the Party.

There is one other organization that should be mentioned, and that is the Non-European Unity Movement (N.E.U.M.), a largely Coloured organization, which, under the impact of countless rebuffs and rejections, rejects in its turn any co-operation with organizations with which white people have anything to do, and whose members try to maintain what is almost impossible in South Africa, namely the abstention from almost every human activity, except one in which they can fully participate. It is a boycott organization on the grand scale, and certainly does not reject suffering as an integral element in such boycotting. But such suffering is not remedial, and does great damage to personality, especially when the suffering, though not rejected, is resented. Here again we touch on the profound problem of the relationship of politics to temperament and experience. The opposition of the N.E.U.M. extends to the Congresses also, and they have angrily obstructed the Indian Congress campaign against the Group Areas Act, because the Congress collaborated with the Liberal Party. How I wish that the N.E.U.M. could overcome this bitter isolationism, and could overcome their prejudice against the white skins of the arrogant 'herrenvolk', and co-operate with other anti-Nationalist forces!

CHAPTER X

CONCLUSION

IF one thing should have emerged from this essay it is this. There is nothing stable about the South African political situation. It has its moments of apparent calm but, underneath, rages a torrent, driven this way and that by a host of conflicting currents and pressures. The sources of the torrent and its diverse currents lie far back in the history of South Africa's people. And, as I have stressed, without some knowledge of this past there can be no understanding South Africa's present and no planning for its future.

What is that future to be? Nobody can tell. For anyone of a liberal persuasion, that future can only be worthwhile if it produces a society in which men can live freely, secure in the knowledge that all those rights which touch most closely upon their everyday lives are safeguarded.

How will Liberals try to guide South Africa's footsteps towards this desirable future?

They will have to confront the intellectual total *apartheid* Afrikaners, some of whom are quite honest in their self-deception, with the total impracticability of their pipe-dream. They will have to confront them with the endless cruelties which the preparations for the *apartheid* state already inflict on African, Indian and Coloured people.

They will have to persuade white opponents of the

Nationalist régime that they have no hope whatsoever of defeating this Government merely by opposing it every five years at elections whose results are foregone conclusions. The Nationalists can only be beaten by a large and well-organized non-racial opposition. It is in such an opposition that all anti-Nationalists should be found, however difficult some of them may find it to take the first, far-reaching step.

White South Africans must continually be reminded of the fact that they can expect no privileged position for their children in the future. Their great fear is that the wheel will turn full circle and that black privilege will replace white. Somehow they must be wakened to the fact that their present intransigence is the most likely cause of what they fear most. Somehow they must be made to realize that they have much more to gain than they can possibly lose by getting rid of the colour bar once and for all. It is Liberals who must bring them to their senses.

[The Liberal Party will have to persuade South Africa—black and white—that a non-racial democracy is a practical proposition and that it can work. It can best hope to do so if it can produce, within the body of its own organization, a forerunner of that society it strives for.] And it can only do *that* convincingly by building up its own membership and organization and by spreading the range of its influence so widely that no South African can afford to ignore its existence and the pressure of its presence. It will have to do this in the face of a Government whose policy it is to make inter-racial contact more and more difficult and which would like to make inter-racial political contact impossible. It is a tough assignment and no Liberal underestimates the threatening challenge of Dr. Verwoerd. To him inter-racial association is anathema. To the Liberal it is the very lifeblood of the society which he knows must be evolved in South Africa if conflict is to be avoided. All that he hopes is that he will be ready to meet this challenge when it comes. Because, if he is not, the chance to draw potential African Nationalists from the dark and gloomy passages of race exclusiveness into the wider, brighter corridors of multi-racialism, may be lost. The hope for massive evolutionary change in South Africa will have been thrown away and only revolution will remain.

I have said that South African Liberals do not under-estimate the challenges which face them. I have suggested that, on their ability to meet them, may depend the survival in South Africa, and perhaps even in sub-Saharan Africa, of those fundamental values which are sometimes called 'Christian'. But the challenge is not only to South African Liberals and to South African Christians. The challenge faces everyone outside South Africa who cherishes those same values. Every possible support must be given to those in South Africa who today strive to find a way towards a society in which baasskap and privilege and senseless dis-crimination will be skeletons of the past. South Africa's strategic position and her vast resources of vital raw materials shrink into insignificance beside the question of how she solves her racial problems. The people of the outside world will be judged, in the eyes of South African leaders of the future, on how they measure up to this challenge in the next few years. Let the West take note.

►◄

To sum up, therefore, we see the rôle of the Liberal Party as a supporter of the multi-racial and non-racial front, particularly the Multi-Racial Conference, as a collaborator of the Congress movement in all opposition to racial dis crimination, as a supporter of all those who believe in a non-racial democracy, as an exposer of the total-*apartheid* myth, as a home for United Party liberals who have been rejected, as a believer—in spite of the omens—in the possibility of evolutionary change, as an opponent of all forms of exclusive nationalism, as an upholder of constitutional government and the rule of law, and above all as a defender of man against totalitarian authority, indeed as a defender of those inalienable human rights which are the concern of liberals in every country of the world.

IMPORTANT BACKGROUND
INFORMATION

1. *Estimated Population* 1958 African   9 2/3 million
                                  European   3   ,,
                                  Coloured 1 1/3 ,,
                                  Indian   2/5   ,,

                                  Total   14 2/5 million

2. *Prime Ministers of the Union of South Africa*

1910–1919 General Louis Botha: leader of the South African Party, standing largely for reconciliation between Briton and Afrikaner.

1919–1924 General Smuts: on the death of Botha made leader of the South African Party, which now, menaced by the growth of General Hertzog's Nationalist Party, absorbed the largely English-speaking Unionist Party.

1924 General Hertzog: leader of the Nationalist Party, came to power with the aid of the largely English-speaking Labour Party.

1933 General Hertzog joined forces with General Smuts and became leader of the new United Party. Dr. Malan led the break-away Nationalist Party.

1939 General Smuts defeated General Hertzog on a motion calling for active intervention by South Africa in the Second World War, and became the new Prime Minister and leader of the United Party. General Hertzog died soon after.

1948 Dr. Malan and his Nationalist Party came to power.

1952 Mr. Strijdom became Prime Minister and new leader of the Nationalist Party on Dr. Malan's retirement.

1958 Mr. Strijdom died on August 24, and was succeeded by his most extreme supporter, Dr. F. H. Verwoerd. The change in premiership does not disturb, but gives added force to the closing arguments of the book.

INDEX